Teasing, Tattling, Defiance *and More*

Positive Approaches to 10 Common Classroom Behaviors

MARGARET BERRY WILSON

NORTHEAST FOUNDATION FOR CHILDREN, INC.

The stories in this book are all based on real events in the classroom. However, to respect the privacy of students, names and identifying characteristics have been changed.

All net proceeds from the sale of this book support the work of Northeast Foundation for Children, Inc. (NEFC). NEFC, a not-for-profit educational organization, is the developer of the *Responsive Classroom*® approach to teaching.

ISBN 978-1-892989-54-3
Library of Congress Control Number: 2012952219

Cover and book design by Helen Merena
Cover illustration ©Lynn Zimmerman, Lucky Dog Designs. All rights reserved.

Northeast Foundation for Children, Inc.
85 Avenue A, P.O. Box 718
Turners Falls, MA 01376-0718

800-360-6332
www.responsiveclassroom.org

Third printing 2014

CONTENTS

INTRODUCTION

Children calling out during discussions, showing petty meanness to classmates, staring off into space during lessons—often, it's these little day-to-day misbehaviors that can make teaching difficult and sometimes even prompt us teachers to question our career choice. It's easy to feel as if there's nothing we can do about students' behavior. But with the proper strategies, patience, and caring, we can guide children to succeed in school.

In fact, it was when I realized this truth and came to see children's behavior as something I *could* influence—and that doing so was an essential part of my role, not just an annoying distraction—that I truly began to love teaching. I wrote this book to help you embrace this same idea and find ever more fulfillment from teaching children. In this book, I'll show you how to use a proven approach to discipline that will enable you to deal positively and successfully with ten common classroom behaviors that can get in the way of learning:

- Listening & attention challenges
- Teasing & name calling
- Cliques & exclusion
- Tattling
- Defiance
- Disengagement & lack of motivation
- Silliness & showing off
- Too much physical contact
- Dishonesty
- Frustration & meltdowns

Discipline is like any other subject—something to be taught. Just as we teach children *how* to read before *expecting* them to read, we also need to set behavior expectations and teach children how to meet those expectations. And when children make a behavior mistake, we need to respond with learning in mind—not shame or punishment—just as we would if they made a mistake in reading.

When we approach discipline this way, children do better in school. Their behavior improves, which in turn enables them to do better socially and academically. As they see these positive results, they become even more engaged in learning and deepen their relationships with us and their classmates—resulting in further improvements and growth.

I hope this book serves as your go-to guide for common behavior challenges and inspires you in helping students.

Why Do Children Misbehave?

In the classic picture book *Curious George Visits the Library*, George is waiting for story hour. He's excited and ready to listen. At first, George is quite attentive as the librarian reads a book about bunnies. However, George notices that she has a book about dinosaurs in her line-up and he becomes anxious for her to read that one.

When she instead reads a book about trains next, his patience fails him: "George tried to sit quietly and wait for the dinosaur book to be read. But sometimes it is hard for a little monkey to be patient." George grabs the dinosaur book and runs off.

Whenever I read this book, I'm reminded that all of us, children and adults, are striving to behave the best we can, but sometimes circumstances conspire against us. At school, children want to behave and learn, but they may have unmet needs or not yet have developed the necessary skills—academically or socially—to succeed.

Perhaps, like Curious George, a student's patience and self-control are not yet strong enough to enable her to resist temptation. Or a child may not know how to take turns and share materials so he "misbehaves" during work times. A student who feels disconnected from her classmates may try to remedy the situation by socializing when she's supposed to be listening.

A student who finds an assignment too challenging may disrupt the class or refuse to do the work to avoid failing. Even physical needs can come into play: A child who's hungry or tired will have a much harder time exercising the willpower it takes to maintain positive behavior.

Throughout this book, I encourage you to look at children's behavior through two lenses: first, children want to and can learn to behave positively, and second, when they make mistakes with their behavior it's because, like Curious George, certain factors have gotten in their way.

By understanding these factors, we can tailor our instruction so that children can better develop the willpower, self-discipline, and other key skills they need to meet expectations and focus on learning. Understanding the possible reasons for children's misbehavior doesn't mean excusing it. Rather, it means having empathy for children when they misstep and holding firm to expectations for behavior at school.

The reasons behind any human behavior are complex, but we can think of children's misbehavior as generally arising from these main influences:

1 ✳ *basic needs*

2 ✳ *social-emotional needs*

3 ✳ *lack of social-emotional skills*

4 ✳ *lack of academic skills*

5 ✳ *developmental factors*

I discuss these five influences in greater detail in Chapters 1 through 10. For now, here's a brief overview.

1 ✳ To Meet Basic Needs

Is the child hungry? Tired? Fidgety?

We all need food, water, rest, and physical movement. If we're hungry or tired, or have been sitting for too long, our willpower—our ability to be patient, talk respectfully, and follow the rules—weakens and our behavior suffers accordingly.

One year I taught a student who began each day in a foul mood. Thomas entered grumpily, barely talked to classmates, and took quick offense if I "bothered" him. As the year went on, I began to notice that Thomas's mood picked up considerably after snack. I had one of those "aha" moments: he was hungry! I started making sure he ate as soon as our day started as well as several times throughout the day, and the change in Thomas was remarkable. Since then, I've wondered how many children whom I had considered temperamental really just needed to eat.

For some children, not having enough opportunities for physical activity is the culprit. As they squirm in their seats, fiddle with objects, and whisper to classmates, it's like watching their willpower evaporate.

When I first taught, I set up the schedule to begin with a morning meeting, then calendar time, followed by a writing mini-lesson. Although I included some interactivity, I also had students sitting in the exact same spots on the rug. Students started off well enough, but when it came time for writing, their focus waned and disruptive behaviors increased. The problem was not their behavior, but the schedule. They needed more chances to move.

Unfulfilled physical needs will not always explain children's behavior. But when they misstep, we should begin with the basics—by checking whether their physical needs are being met.

2 * To Meet Social-Emotional Needs

Children's social and emotional needs are also strong motivators of their behavior. We can think of children's (and adults') social-emotional needs as falling into three basic categories:

- ***a need for belonging***
- ***a need for significance***
- ***a need for fun***

These three needs drive many of children's behaviors—whom they choose to play with, how they respond to expectations and teacher directions, how they handle setbacks … the list goes on. Often when children misbehave, they're sending us a message that one or more of these needs aren't being met.

Does the child feel a sense of belonging?

It's a familiar classroom scene: Four second grade girls start a club at recess and begin to plan some adventures. But soon their focus shifts to creating elaborate entrance requirements, which they use to turn away all others.

All of us have a powerful, innate need to belong to a group. Early in life, this need is usually met within our family. As we go through school, our network of groups expands. We make new friends, play on teams, and take part in other school activities. In these groups, we're trying to fit in and find our place in the world. We may even wear the same types of clothes our friends wear, use the same slang, and exclude others to cement our standing in the group.

This need to belong drives human behaviors in both positive and negative ways. On the positive side, children reach out to those in their groups. They try to get to know them better and bond with them. They often follow rules to feel accepted in the classroom community.

On the negative side, the need to belong can lead children to break rules. When their teachers are talking, they may engage in side conversations to connect with those around them. They might join in on teasing if the child doing the teasing is someone they want to be friends with. Forming cliques appeals to many children because it helps them feel like they belong to a special group.

And when a few students start breaking the rule that prohibits running in the hallways, it shouldn't surprise us when other children join in the fun. The age-old defense—"everyone's doing it"—really stems from our inner drive to belong and be like everyone else. As children try to please classmates and attract allies, they'll often break rules and ignore expectations.

Does the child feel significant?

It's not always sufficient for children to feel they're part of a group. They're also likely to have an inner drive to feel that they're important to that group. This often leads children to go out of their way to help their teachers and classmates. It motivates many students to excel in art, music, academics, athletics, or the social arena. Yet the need to feel significant, including having some autonomy and power, can also lead children to make mistakes with their behavior.

Sometimes breaking a rule helps children feel a sense of significance—"You can't make me do that. I'll do what I want." Or it's a way to get their classmates to notice them—"Hey everyone, watch this!"

For example, as students enter a sixth grade classroom, the teacher directs them to go to their seats and get out their journals for an opening reflection. One student asks, "Why can't we start with a game the way Ms. Howard does?" While his classmates start writing, he sits with arms crossed. Later, as others share their reflections, he scoffs, "That's stupid." And so it goes for the entire day. This student wants to let his teachers and classmates know that he is important and has power. He's striving to be noticed—and it's working.

Does the child have opportunities for fun?

A third grade boy with a talent for paper-folding turns his math worksheet into a frog. Pretty soon, the frog is hopping around his desk. Then, flick. It lands on a classmate's desk and she flicks it back. Flick, flick, flick, they continue to play—until math is forgotten. Why? The short answer is that the worksheet was boring.

All children need to have fun at school, and fun can take many different forms. Sometimes, it involves laughing and joking with others, or engaging in free play. At other times, it means being fully engrossed in an assignment or project because it's relevant and connected to their lives.

When the work doesn't feel engaging, children will find ways to make it that way. They'll doodle, crack jokes, rush through assignments, and much, much more. In short, if school isn't fun, children will find ways to fix that problem!

3 * A Lack of Social-Emotional Skills

What social-emotional skills does the child need to learn?

All of us had to learn the social skills that we now use automatically in our lives: saying a friendly "Good morning" to a colleague at work, thanking a friend for a favor, and so on. None of us was born knowing how to do these things.

Children often struggle at school because they haven't yet learned the social-emotional skills required for success there. For many children, school is their first chance to learn these skills. No wonder they blurt out "He smells bad." "She's fat." "I'm first!" They may hit someone who hits them or says something they don't like because they haven't learned how to solve conflicts with words or by seeking out an adult. Even well into the upper elementary grades, some children are still developing basic skills such as listening and focusing.

It takes time for children to learn, try out, and master social-emotional skills, especially ones such as perspective taking, active listening, and empathy that may be just beyond their current abilities. The good news for teachers is that children are capable of incredible growth and can learn these skills at any age—as long as we provide them with the teaching and practice they need.

4 ✳ A Lack of Academic Skills

What academic (or cognitive) skills does the child need to learn?

I once heard an educational speaker say that a child would rather appear bad than stupid. In other words, some children's misbehavior is a conscious effort to hide the difficulties they're having academically.

Consider a student who struggles with reading. She may work very hard to distract those around her, engage in side conversations, or "lose" her materials. She may even interrupt the teacher's work with other students to complain that there are no books she likes in the classroom library or that someone else has the book she needs.

This student may feel so uncomfortable about her inability to read at grade level that she'll do just about anything to avoid failing. For other students, the overall academic requirements of school can feel so overwhelming that their entire day is one long struggle. They may make a mighty effort but still be unsuccessful. For them, misbehavior can result from sheer frustration. They may act out, daydream, or complain that the work is "boring" (often code for "too hard"). And some students may simply not have developed basic, but essential, academic skills such as how to focus on one thing at a time and stick to it.

So when a child is struggling with behavior, ask yourself this question: "Is this child having difficulties academically?" Often, providing extra academic support will make a big difference in a child's behavior.

5 * Developmental Factors

Are there child development factors at play?

Children's behavior is also driven by where they are developmentally. As they grow, their bodies and brains are changing in dramatic ways. They tend to go through some fairly predictable stages, each marked by certain strengths, challenges, and ways of seeing the world. These characteristics can lead children to behave in ways that don't fit school expectations. Thus, behaviors that are developmentally appropriate may look like problematic behaviors to teachers.

For example, six-year-olds are often more socially driven than their five- or seven-year-old counterparts. Developmentally, they need to talk and socialize frequently. If teachers expect long periods of quiet, independent work, these students may struggle meeting expectations. Eleven-year-olds are often moody, self-absorbed, and sensitive, and they care a great deal about what their peers think of them. In the classroom, this means that they'll often take offense at what others say, and they may also appear defiant or skeptical of school rules.

Developmental factors shouldn't be used to excuse any kind of misbehavior. However, teachers need to have a basic understanding of these factors, cultivate empathy for children's pathways of growth and development, and, when possible, adjust their teaching accordingly so that all children have the opportunity to meet the same high expectations.

Chapters 1 through 10 each include a table of child development basics at various grades and ages that are relevant to the specific behavior discussed in that chapter. A word of caution: Although there are general patterns to children's development, every child grows in his or her own unique way. As you read the developmental information in these chapters, keep these ideas in mind:

- ***Human development is complex.*** Most scientists describe the process as a dynamic interaction between a person's biological disposition and environmental factors—including the person's culture and family, school, place of worship, and media exposure. The tables are not intended to ignore this complexity. Instead, they offer you a bridge between child development theory and children's real-life classroom behaviors.
- ***Every child is unique.*** Although most children follow similar general patterns of development, no two children—not even identical twins—will develop in the exact same way or at the same rate. And for many children, one area may develop much faster than another. For example, a kindergartner might have moved past the concrete phase in language development but still struggle with gross motor actions such as skipping and jumping. The tables give you some common characteristics, but they should never limit your thinking about a student's potential.
- ***Use child development information to problem-solve if something puzzling comes up.*** For instance, if you teach fifth graders, you may notice that some students frequently complain about being hungry mid-morning, even though they ate breakfast. Because many fifth graders are experiencing growth spurts, they're using up a lot of energy. As their energy level goes down, so may their ability to focus and maintain other positive behaviors. Knowing this, you might set special guidelines that allow them to have a snack while they work.

- ***Be aware of developmentally younger and older students.*** In any classroom, you'll have students of various ages and at various points along the developmental path. The tallest student in the class may seem younger socially. A student who is younger chronologically may be a stronger reader. Also keep in mind that as the year progresses, you'll most likely see a shift in the class as a whole—springtime students will be a different bunch than they were at the start of school.

The essential goal here is to understand general child development patterns while getting to know your students as individuals. Doing so will enable you to help children reduce behavior mistakes while also promoting their positive behaviors and academic success.

Children With Special Behavior Challenges

Children who have suffered trauma, are under great stress, or have other mental health challenges often exhibit the most challenging behaviors. For example, experiencing a major natural disaster such as Hurricane Katrina or living in a chaotic or dangerous environment can negatively impact children's developing brains, making it much harder for them to learn and maintain self-control.

Children who don't feel safe (in or out of school) may withdraw, appear unmotivated, or lash out when upset. It may often seem like these children are in a "fight or flight" state of mind. And in a sense they are—their survival instinct has gone into hyperdrive, making it hard for them to use the rational part of their brain. Thus, they tend to react to minor setbacks in extreme, instinctual ways.

It's beyond the scope of this book to fully address the specific needs of this population of children. However, many of the strategies discussed can form a crucial part of addressing their challenges, support any specialized help they're receiving, and enable you to establish a positive and supportive learning environment—a bedrock that can make a significant impact in these students' lives.

The Importance of Empathy

Understanding why children misbehave doesn't mean we excuse the behavior. It means instead that we develop empathy for all our students and form stronger bonds with each one. In the process, we'll be better prepared to respond effectively if they slip up and help them build stronger positive behavior skills going forward.

Children have a great capacity to change, including learning new ways of behaving. By doing our best every day to get to know children as individuals, empathetically coach them in developing skills, and help them learn from mistakes, we give them (and ourselves) hope for a brighter future.

The *Responsive Classroom*® Approach to Discipline

For children to learn the habits and skills of positive behavior, we need to teach discipline explicitly, just as we teach math, science, and other academic subjects. And we must do so in ways that address the causes of children's behavior struggles. The *Responsive Classroom* approach to discipline does just that.

Using this approach, you establish high—and achievable—expectations for positive behavior and actively teach children how to meet them. When children make mistakes, as they will, this approach also enables you to respond effectively so that children get back on the learning path as quickly as possible.

In this overview, you'll learn how to:

- ➤ teach positive behavior skills, including teaching children how to meet their own needs in productive ways
- ➤ respond effectively in the moment when misbehavior is taking place, and what to do if the misbehavior continues
- ➤ communicate with students' families respectfully and effectively about behavior issues

The chapters that follow will then help you to apply these strategies to ten common classroom behaviors.

Proactive Strategies

How to Promote Positive Behavior

Often when we seek help with behavior challenges, we just want to know what to do in the moment—when children are actually misbehaving. What we do in the moment obviously will have an immediate effect; it will also have some effect on students' future actions.

Yet, the steps we take *before* challenging situations arise will have a much more powerful and lasting impact on children. The more time we devote to this proactive work, the more skills children will develop and the more they'll be encouraged by the positive effects of their behavior on themselves and others.

This means that we shouldn't wait for children to make a mistake—and only step in at that point. Instead, we need to proactively build a classroom environment that leads to positive behavior and explicitly teach children positive ways to act. In reality, we should be spending a lot more time on this proactive work than on reacting to misbehaviors so that children develop the behavior "muscles" they need for success in school.

Here are the essential proactive steps to take:

- Make sure children's basic needs are being met
- Build a safe, caring community
- Address students' social-emotional needs
- Set students up for academic success
- Establish clear expectations
- Create class rules
- Teach the rules and expectations
- Use positive teacher language

Make sure children's basic needs are being met

When children are hungry, thirsty, tired of sitting still, or distracted by other physical needs, they're less able to maintain self-control. Planning how to meet these needs during the school day is essential to fostering positive behavior and learning.

- ***Water.*** Students need to drink water more often than just at lunch and recess. Do you need to provide water bottles or remind students to bring in their own? Do you provide regular access to water fountains?
- ***Food.*** Students may also need to eat more often than at breakfast and lunch. Think about whether you need to schedule morning and afternoon snack times or provide a working snack time, such as during reading workshop.
- ***Bathroom breaks.*** Do you have a system set up so students can go as needed or take breaks at regular intervals?
- ***Movement.*** Physical activity keeps our blood flowing and stimulates our thinking. Think about how you could include movement in academic lessons. For example, could students stand and partner-chat about an assigned question? Schedule movement breaks throughout the day as well, such as a quick, energizing game, three minutes of yoga or stretching, or a brisk walk.

Build a safe, caring community

When students know that we care about them as individuals—what they like and dislike, what their life outside of school is like, what they hope for and fear—they're much more likely to be cooperative and engaged at school. While they'll still misstep at times, they'll do so less frequently and more readily accept redirection or logical consequences.

The same is true when students form bonds with one another. If students know and trust each other, they'll see how their actions can affect everyone in the classroom, not just the teacher or themselves. When they feel that their classmates care about them, their desire to belong, feel significant, and have fun will shape their behavior in positive ways. Ultimately, when you create a safe, caring classroom community, that environment will bring forth children's best behavior and enable their optimal learning.

- ***Begin each day with a community-building routine,*** such as a morning meeting. You can set this up so that children greet one another, share information about themselves, do an engaging activity, and read a morning message to prepare for the day's learning. Launching the day this way also gives you opportunities to introduce, practice, and reinforce social-emotional and academic skills.
- ***Include community-building activities in academic lessons*** to allow students to get to know one another. For example, you can have them write and share about their daily lives. Or structure a math lesson in which students play a math-facts game with a partner or use manipulatives in small groups to solve problems.
- ***Spend time with students outside of the classroom*** whenever you can. Sit with them at lunch, play with them at recess, and chat with them as they arrive in the morning and when they leave at the end of the day.
- ***Talk to students one-on-one throughout the day.*** Do this for all students, especially those who may push your buttons. They need to know you—and you really need to know them. Try to keep track of whom you've had these conversations with, especially for larger classes, to avoid having some students fall through the cracks.

TEACHING TIP

There's Something to Like in Every Child—We Just Have to Find It

While it's natural to warm up to some children more quickly than others, it's important that we look for qualities and talents to admire in every child. When we know and appreciate each child as an individual, we're better able to respond with empathy and in ways that build up, rather than diminish, the child.

Address students' social-emotional needs

Beyond the community-building strategies just described, there are other important steps to take throughout the day to help children be engaged in their learning and feel that they belong and are valued. When we enable children to meet their social-emotional needs, they'll be much more likely to act in kind, caring, and respectful ways and to achieve academic success.

- ***Provide multiple opportunities for students to interact*** with all their classmates. For example, assign and reassign seats, schedule rotating partners, and vary work groups.
- ***Provide "air time" to all students,*** so everyone has a chance to be heard. For example, use a system for calling on students, such as choosing name cards. Give students frequent opportunities to share opinions and ask questions in whole-group, small-group, and paired discussions.
- ***Respond equitably to students.*** Children are always watching us, so even subtle signs can lead some children to feel more or less significant than others. When we respond "Great idea!" to one child but just give a quick nod to another, we may send an unintended message that we value certain children over others.
- ***Have fun with students.*** I recently saw a teacher playing tag with students at recess. The joy she exhibited had a visible effect on them, both during and after recess. When we're playful and we make learning fun, we model for children how they can do this for themselves—and we create an environment where fun and play are natural and productive parts of learning.

Set students up for academic success

If children are bored in school or struggling with their learning, they may act out or withdraw. For example, a student who is having difficulties with an assignment may tease others or act silly in an attempt to deflect her frustration.

- ***Consider where children are developmentally.*** For instance, think about how much information they can take in through listening before needing to talk or move, or whether they'll need something concrete, such as a demonstration, to understand an abstract concept.
- ***Connect lessons to students' interests and prior knowledge.*** Students do best when they can connect what they're learning to their lives. If they're learning about social classes during a unit on the Middle Ages, you might have students reflect on a time when someone else seemed to have more social status than they did. Or use a topic that interests students, such as sports, popular culture, or current events, to draw them into a lesson.
- ***Name the learning objective of the lesson.*** When students understand the purpose of a lesson or activity, they're more likely to stay focused and persevere.
- ***Differentiate.*** Students remain more engaged when they're working at their appropriate level of skill and challenge. As best you can, meet students' varied academic needs by offering alternative or modified assignments. For instance, give students multiple learning choices throughout the school week. For students who are struggling academically, consider providing more hands-on activities and opportunities to work with peer helpers.

Establish clear expectations

Students do better when they know exactly how they're supposed to act at school, and why. We can't assume that children know these things, because school expectations often differ from those outside of school. Even with older students, don't expect that they will automatically know how to behave. This year's expectations might be the same as last year's, but students need to know that. And if expectations are different, they really need to know that!

- ***Make expectations clear from day one.*** On the first day of school, establish that this classroom is a safe place, where everyone is to be treated with kindness and respect.

➤ ***Model and practice key routines.*** During the first few weeks, teach the routines students will be using all year long. Pay attention to the little details of these procedures. If you expect children to line up in a straight line along the left side of the room, say so—and show exactly how that should look and sound. You may even want to take a photo of the ideal line and post it near the door as a visual reminder.

An effective way to teach, model, and practice skills and routines is to use Interactive Modeling, a quickly paced, seven-step teaching practice.

The 7 Steps of Interactive Modeling:

1. Say what you will model and why.
2. Model the behavior.
3. Ask students what they notice.
4. Invite one or more students to model.
5. Again, ask students what they noticed.
6. Have all students practice.
7. Provide feedback.

See pages 24–25 for more information.

➤ ***Provide extra support as needed.*** Some students will enter our class not yet having learned certain skills. Just as we provide extra help for students struggling with academic skills, we need to do the same for those working on behavior skills—such as by giving extra reminders and reinforcements.

Create class rules

A set of class rules makes expectations clear and serves as a guide for children, helping them to skillfully navigate through school. It can be especially powerful to create these rules together with students. You can do this early in the year by discussing what their learning goals are and what rules will help everyone reach those goals.

Creating rules together builds community, cultivates students' sense of belonging and significance, and helps students become more invested in following the rules. Students see that doing so is good for everyone—not because "the teacher said so," but because "we all think so!"

Whether you engage in the rule-making process with students or provide a set of rules for them, class rules are most effective when they:

- ***State a few global ideals.*** When rules are stated globally—such as "Be kind and respectful to everyone" and "Take care of our classroom"—we can rely on them to cover any challenge that may arise. By contrast, if we try to have specific rules that cover every situation ("hands to self in line," "share markers," and so on), we'll surely fail because we can't anticipate everything, and savvy students may claim that their behavior fell outside a rule's narrow parameters ("I didn't know I had to pick trash up off the floor").

- ***Encourage reasoned thinking and discussion.*** When the rules state global ideals, they give children opportunities to think through how they should act in various situations. Providing opportunities for such reasoned reflection is the essence of teaching discipline. With globally stated rules in place, we can lead children in discussing what following the rules looks, sounds, and feels like in everyday situations, such as when someone wants to join a game at recess, when they get frustrated with an assignment, or when there aren't enough supplies to go around.

- ***Tell children what to do, not what not to do.*** Negative rules such as "don't be mean" offer children little guidance for how to behave. If they're not supposed to be mean, what should they do? Having positively stated rules only—such as "Be kind to and respectful of others"—not only answers this question, but paints images of positive rather than negative behaviors in children's minds.

- ***Are easy to remember.*** Limit the number of rules to three to five. Write them in child-friendly language to make it easier for everyone to remember. For example, instead of "Your academic achievement is your responsibility," try "Take care of our own learning."

➤ ***Cover three categories of action.*** To ensure that rules are comprehensive, think in terms of these three categories:

1 **TAKING CARE OF OURSELVES**

You'll want at least one rule to help children realize that they need to take care of their own needs as learners. For example: "Stay focused and do your best work."

2 **TAKING CARE OF EACH OTHER**

A rule about caring for each other will help foster a sense of mutual respect in the classroom and throughout the school. For example: "Be kind to everyone."

3 **TAKING CARE OF THE ENVIRONMENT**

It's also helpful to have a rule that covers children's responsibilities to take care of the physical environment of their classroom and school. For example: "Keep our school clean and safe."

Once the rules are set, display them proudly as a ready reference.

Teach the rules and expectations

It's not enough to display the rules or let them become just another poster. Instead, children need to be taught what it looks, sounds, and feels like to follow the rules in real-life situations.

If a rule says "Take care of each other," how do children follow that, for instance, at recess? How should children respond when someone says something hurtful to them or a friend? What does it look like to follow that rule when working in a group? These are not easy questions to answer. Children need us to teach them how to follow the rules, all year long, not just at the start of school.

Here are three especially powerful techniques for teaching children the rules:

➤ ***Structured reflection.*** Guide students to reflect on questions like the ones on page 23. For example, ask, "What's it going to look and sound like to take care of each other and our substitute teacher tomorrow?" You might want to list students' answers, using a chart like this:

How will we follow our class rule of taking care of each other when we have a substitute?		
Looks like	**Sounds like**	**Feels like**
• Listening and raising hands • Doing what sub asks • Focusing on our work • Helping each other remember our class rules if we forget	• Kind words and same volume as when Mr. R is here • Respectful words and tone • Conversation focused on the discussion topic	• Similar to when Mr. R is here • Calm • Safe • Peaceful • Relaxed

➤ ***Interactive Modeling.*** Interactive Modeling is an effective technique for teaching routines, procedures, and skills that need to be done in a specific way, such as how to line up for the bus, shut down a computer, or have a partner chat about a question the teacher poses. In contrast to lecturing or traditional modeling, Interactive Modeling creates a clear mental image of the expected behavior, fully engages students in noticing details about it, and gives them immediate opportunities to practice it and receive teacher feedback. For an example of an Interactive Modeling lesson, see the next page.

➤ ***Role-play.*** Role-play, unlike Interactive Modeling, helps students apply the rules to complex situations that could be handled in any number of ways, such as what to do if someone invites you to join a clique and you really want to, but you also know it's wrong to exclude others. In a role-play, the teacher partially acts out a concrete scenario with one or more students. She then freezes the action at a crucial decision point, and students brainstorm the various ways the person in the scenario could act to meet the rules. Next, students take turns acting out and observing what their various solutions would look like in action.

Interactive Modeling in Action: How to Admit You Were Dishonest

1 ***Say what you will model and why*** **•** "Our class rules say that we will 'respect each other.' One way to do that is to tell people when you said something that wasn't true. I'm going to show you what it looks like to admit to saying something untrue. See what you notice."

2 ***Model the behavior*** **•** Invite a student to be the listener. Turn toward him, look him in the eye, and say: "Sean, I told you I had a rock collection and that's not true. I shouldn't have said that. I'm sorry."

3 ***Ask students what they noticed*** **•** "What did you notice about the way I told Sean I had said something untrue?" If needed, ask prompting questions to bring out key aspects of your demonstration that students may not have noticed. For example: "What were my eyes doing? What kind of voice did I use?"

4 ***Invite one or more students to model the same behavior*** **•** Who can demonstrate how to admit to someone that they made up a story about a rock collection in the same way I did?"

5 ***Again, ask students what they noticed*** **•** "What did you notice about the way Sanji told DeMarcus that she had said something untrue?"

6 ***Have all students practice*** **•** Assign students partners and have them take turns practicing the same behavior.

7 ***Provide feedback*** **•** "I noticed everyone faced their partner and made eye contact. It takes courage to admit you said something untrue. Because we've practiced this today, I'm confident that in real situations you'll be more able to show that courage."

For in-depth guidance on using Interactive Modeling, see Interactive Modeling: A Powerful Technique for Teaching Children *by Margaret Berry Wilson (Northeast Foundation for Children, 2012) and www.responsiveclassroom.org/what-interactive-modeling.*

Use positive teacher language

Some of our most powerful teaching tools are our words and tone of voice. By using these tools effectively, we can help children develop self-control, a sense of community, and academic skills. The following two types of teacher language are especially effective in proactively teaching positive behavior.

1 REMINDING LANGUAGE

If you know that a particular time of day is going to be challenging for students, take a minute to remind them of the expectations and how class rules apply to that situation. For instance, before recess, ask, "Who can tell us one way we can follow our class rule to 'Be safe' at recess?" Invite several students to answer based on what they know from your prior teaching. Before a tricky transition, you might say, "It's time to return to your tables and begin writing workshop. Use our chart to help you be prepared to write." For reminders to work best, be sure to:

- ***Keep them brief.*** Reminders work best when they're brief statements or questions and reflect the expectations or rules. Be clear, simple, and direct.
- ***Use a matter-of-fact tone and neutral body language.*** Students will be more engaged and open to the reminders if you're genuine and respectful about the need for them. If, instead, your tone implies that you're annoyed that you have to spend your time on the issue, students will respond with less interest and maybe even defiance.
- ***Prompt students to recall the expectations.*** Reminders are often more powerful when students have to recall the key expectations themselves. For example, you might prompt students to recall recess rules by asking, "Who can remind us how we'll take care of each other at recess?" rather than telling them, "Remember to tap gently when playing tag." Students are also more likely to remember key aspects of behavior when they hear reminders from each other, rather than just from their teacher.

2 REINFORCING LANGUAGE

To foster student success and support your proactive work, it's critical to notice—and to tell students you noticed—that they're on the right track. If they hear you pointing out their efforts and successes, they're more likely to repeat those in the future.

For reinforcing language to be most effective, follow these guidelines:

- ***Name concrete behaviors.*** Generic phrases such as "awesome" or "good job" fail to teach children what they did well. Instead, children need to hear exactly what they did well because it gives them specific information about how to be successful again. For instance, you might tell a student who's working on letting people finish speaking before jumping in, "I saw you listening to other people during our classroom discussion. You looked at them and let them speak. That's exactly what we've been practicing."
- ***Use a warm, professional tone.*** Feedback has the strongest impact when the recipient feels that it's genuine. When students hear us speak to them in a friendly, respectful tone, they feel our sincerity, whereas a flat, patronizing, or overexcited tone can make our feedback sound fake or manipulative.
- ***Give feedback directly to the recipient(s) only.*** When you want to give positive feedback to the whole class, speak to them globally and name exactly what they all did well. For example: "Everyone worked together to clean the lunchroom quickly. Those tables were spotless and ready for the next class!"

  If you want to reinforce one student's efforts, however, speak to him in private. Avoid saying to the whole class, "I like the way James has his hand up to speak," hoping to get everyone to raise their hands. That kind of public recognition may embarrass the student and feel manipulative to others. Instead, whisper to James, "I see that you're following our guidelines for participating in discussions. You raised your hand each time you wanted to speak."

- ***Avoid using words of personal approval, such as "I like."*** Children need to know that following rules helps them and their classmates learn together. When you use "I like the way you . . ." you imply a different goal for following rules—to make you happy. Even though you may indeed be pleased, making teachers happy is not the point of following the rules.

  Strive to give positive feedback using neutral terms, such as "I noticed," "I heard," or "I saw." Or leave the "I" out entirely. For example: "You all remembered to keep side conversations to a minimum. That gave us more time to share and get to know each other."

  Shifting away from the language of personal approval can be hard, but with practice it can become second nature.

Reactive Strategies

How to Respond Effectively When Children Misbehave

Even with the best proactive work, children will sometimes still break rules and fail to meet expectations. When they do, we need to respond quickly, effectively, and nonpunitively. We want to stop behavior mistakes from escalating, restore the children to positive behavior as soon as possible, and keep other students' learning on track.

The goals for responding to misbehavior are to:

- Stop the rule-breaking behavior
- Maintain a safe, orderly classroom
- Help students recognize and repair any damage their mistake caused
- Help students develop internal control of their behavior
- Preserve the dignity of the individual and group

To meet these goals, here's a menu of options you can choose from:

- Use nonverbal cues
- Move closer to the student
- Use positive teacher language
- Use a logical consequence

Depending on the situation and student, you might choose different options at different times to address the same misbehavior.

Use nonverbal cues

This simple technique lets students know right away when they're going off track. For example, if a student is chatting while someone else is speaking, put your finger to your lips as a silent reminder to listen. If a student reaches for a math manipulative while you're still giving directions, a simple shake of the head can be enough to help her remember to wait until you're finished. Often, just a knowing look will help students stop and return their focus to the lesson or task at hand. To make the most of these visual reminders:

- ***Use them democratically.*** If you use these reminders with just a few students, they may ignore you or think you're targeting them.
- ***Teach their meaning.*** Teach students what your primary nonverbal signals mean and what they should do when they see them. You may even want to post a chart and let students use these signals as gentle reminders with each other.
- ***Keep them respectful.*** If you're vigorously shaking your head and scowling at a student who wants to gather art supplies before it's time, she may stop, but she's more likely to feel embarrassed or rebellious than cooperative. If instead you make direct eye contact and gently shake your head, she'll likely stop and take your signal as just a reminder, helping her to pull back from a misstep.

Move closer to the student

Although it can be tempting to stay in one spot and try to direct your classroom from there, the simple act of moving closer to a student or group of students (also referred to as using proximity) will often restore positive behavior quickly. In some situations, students may not be able to see us for a visual cue to work. By moving closer to them, we can help them remember expectations. For instance, when a small group veers off task to talk about last night's TV show, a teacher's presence is often all they need to return to work.

Occasionally, students may be so engrossed in what they're doing that they don't sense your presence. Rather than taking this as a sign that they're intentionally ignoring you, once you're close to them, quietly tell them exactly what they should be doing.

Use positive teacher language

In certain situations, a verbal reminder or a redirection is what's needed to help a student stop a negative behavior and return to positive behavior. Timing is important here. If you notice a student is just starting to go off course—for instance, a student is starting to struggle with listening or is about to reach for something off limits—give a reminder. When students are already engaging in a rule-breaking behavior, give a redirection.

Reminders and redirections work best when you:

- ***Affirm your belief in children's ability to regain control.*** Whenever we speak to children, we want to send the message that we believe they can succeed. This message is communicated through our choice of words. For example, "Show me how we practiced being a respectful partner" says we know they can recall these skills. "Remind me what our rule says about . . ." says we believe they know the rules and expectations.
- ***Are nonjudgmental in word and tone.*** When children hear words that suggest dislike, shame, or condemnation, they're likely to react in negative ways (just as adults would). Instead of saying in a harsh tone,

"You're being rude and disrespectful," use a calm, even voice: "Stop. Our classroom rule says we will use kind words." The more neutral our words and tone, the more effective we'll be.

TEACHING TIP

Words to Avoid When Responding to Misbehavior

"Why did you . . . ?" Children typically can't answer this question in the heat of the moment.

"You always (or you never) . . ." This tells children that they can't change, which decreases their motivation to try: *If I always lie, why try to be honest?*

"Why am I not surprised?" This implies that children are predestined to behave a certain way. It sets them (and us) up for failure. Children need to hear that we expect their best, so that they can expect the best of themselves, too.

- ***Stress the deed, not the doer.*** Compare "Stop, Tina, hands to yourself. Try again." with "Stop, Tina. You forgot to keep your hands to yourself—again." The first example says "Everyone messes up. You made a mistake. Here's how to fix it." The second example comments more on the child's character and sends a very different and discouraging message: "You're a problem child. Something is wrong with you."

- ***Are short, clear, and direct.*** When children are upset or off track, their self-control and ability to process information are weakened. They're not in a state of mind to listen to lectures or answer questions. So, when you remind or redirect students, be as succinct as possible: "Stop pushing and move away from each other" or "Stop. Walk."

- ***Strike a balance between being matter-of-fact and kind.*** When reminding or redirecting students, we'll have the greatest impact when our voices, tone, and body language demonstrate both empathy and authority: We care about the student and we mean what we say. To a student who's upset about having to stop work on an engaging assignment, we might say, "I know how much you love drawing, but it's time to stop now. Take two minutes to finish up and then join us on the rug."

Reminding and Redirecting Language in Action	
Instead of this	**Try this**
"Why are you two always so messy? I have to remind you every day to clean up."	"Both of you need to go back and clean up the area where you were working."
"You were really careless with this work. It's full of errors."	"Before you hand this in, proofread it and see how many errors you can fix."
"You are such chatterboxes—you talk all day long! I need you to stop and listen."	"Voices off." (Then pause to make sure they are.) "Eyes on me."

Use a logical consequence

When children need more than a reminder or redirection, a logical consequence can help them connect their behavior to its effects and repair any damage their behavior may have caused. Unlike punishments, logical consequences are respectful of children, realistic for them to carry out, and relevant to the behavior. The three types to consider using are:

1 ***Loss of privilege.*** When a child isn't following classroom expectations during an activity, a logical consequence might be that she temporarily loses the privilege of doing that activity. For instance, if a child doesn't work cooperatively with a group, she might have to work on her own for the rest of the period. Or if a child fools around and spills water all over the bathroom, he might lose the privilege of going to the bathroom independently for a while.

However, it's not a logical consequence for a child to lose a privilege that's unrelated to the problematic behavior. For example, a child shouldn't lose recess for talking out of turn. Such a loss of privilege can feel punitive (which, in turn, can lead to further misbehavior).

A loss of privilege can also feel punitive if it lasts too long. Once the child demonstrates readiness to handle the responsibility, it's important to restore the privilege.

2 ***Reparation ("You break it, you fix it").*** Sometimes children need to make amends for their behavior. If a child isn't paying attention and tips over his lunch tray, for example, the consequence may be that he has to clean up the mess. A child who accidentally deletes her and her partner's computer work needs to find a way to recreate their work.

One caution: Children should only have to make amends that directly relate to and are in proportion to what they did. If a child writes on her desk, it's a logical consequence to clean that desk. However, if she has to miss lunch or spend time with the custodian cleaning the entire classroom, she will likely feel punished.

3 ***Positive time-out.*** At times, the most effective way to stop a child's missteps and restore positive behavior is to direct him to take a short break. The purpose of the break is for the child to regroup mentally and emotionally and regain self-control. For example, if a child has interrupted another student and you sense that a reminder or redirection won't be enough, you might say, "Mary, time-out" or "Freddy, take a break."

To make sure time-out does not feel punitive to students, use Interactive Modeling to carefully teach its purpose and how it will be used. (See the table on page 34 for what to teach students about time-out.) Make sure that time-out is used for all students, not just a few, and that a child's duration in it is short, generally about one to three minutes.

Time-out works most effectively for small disruptions or when you notice early signs that a child is off track. In these instances, time-out gives the child the best chance of calming down and preparing to re-engage with learning. You may also want to check in with the child later to make sure she understands why she went to time-out and what might help her meet expectations next time.

What to Teach Students About Time-Out

- **The purpose of time-out**—for example: "We all break rules at times. When you break a rule, it's my job to keep you and everyone else safe. One way I might do that is to send you to time-out. Time-out is a way for you to regain self-control and keep everyone learning."
- **How to go to time-out**—how to walk calmly to the designated time-out spot and sit down there
- **What to do in time-out**—simple strategies for calming down, such as deep breathing
- **When and how to return from time-out**—how students return on their own, or after a timer goes off or the teacher gives a signal
- **What others should do when someone else is in time-out**—how to stay focused on their work, not the student going to time-out

Have a buddy teacher or other back-up plan

If a child refuses to go to time-out or disrupts others while there, you'll need a back-up plan. You can set up a buddy teacher arrangement for just these situations. Using a buddy teacher lets the child know that consequences have meaning. It also gives him (and you) time to calm down, and it allows you to keep teaching. Here's how the buddy teacher process works:

- ***Agree to be buddy teachers with a colleague.*** You may also wish to have a back-up buddy teacher.
- ***Teach your class about the process.*** Explain that the purpose of going with the buddy teacher is to help a child calm down and return ready to learn. You can use Interactive Modeling to show how to go with the buddy teacher and what to do when a classmate leaves with, and returns from, the buddy teacher.

➤ ***In the moment of need, send someone for the buddy teacher.*** If a student has refused to go to time-out or accept another consequence, calmly send another student with a note to get the buddy teacher. (If there's a paraprofessional in the classroom, you could send him or her instead.) If possible, keep teaching and don't engage further with the child.

➤ ***When the buddy teacher arrives, she escorts the child to her classroom.*** The buddy teacher does not try to problem-solve or have a conversation with the child. Her job is just to keep the child safe.

➤ ***In the buddy teacher's room, the child sits quietly.*** The child uses simple strategies for calming down, such as deep breathing, just as he would in time-out in his own classroom. There is no conversation or problem-solving with the buddy teacher.

➤ ***After a short while, go to the buddy room for the child.*** Welcome the child back into the class as you walk with him and get him started on what he missed. Clear your mind of any resentment so you can offer the child a fresh start.

➤ ***Later in the day, check in with the student.*** Explore with the child what happened, what might have helped, and what he can do differently next time.

More Tips for Responding to Misbehavior

➤ ***Maintain your composure.*** Children's emotions often mirror ours. If we speak impatiently or disrespectfully, that's often how they'll respond to us. When we remain calm, they're more likely to do the same.

➤ ***Respond early to signs of problematic behavior.*** Many teachers ignore a child's first behavior mistake because they hope that it will go away on its own. Unfortunately, minor misbehaviors tend to escalate, so intervene early to nip them in the bud. This minimizes classroom disruptions and makes it easier for children to restore themselves to positive behavior.

- ***Don't take rule-breaking behavior personally.*** Children's behavior, positive or negative, often feels personal to us. In fact, it rarely has anything to do with us. So remember to separate how you feel from how you respond. Some teachers use reminders to help themselves stay calm, such as Q-Tip (Quit Taking It Personally); others use deep breathing or visualization.
- ***Maintain "clean slates" for all children.*** Children shouldn't have to lug around a heavy suitcase filled with their every misdeed. Try to keep any prior mistakes in the past, even when repeated. Avoid phrases such as "Again?" and "How many times . . . ?"
- ***Be fair.*** All children break rules, so when they see us responding to everyone's rule-breaking behaviors, not just to those of certain children, they're more likely to respect our in-the-moment response. Singling out certain children, even if done unintentionally, makes those students more likely to question us and damages our relationship with them.

Remember, when a child is in the middle of misbehaving, it's not the time to teach her what we expect. Instead, stop the behavior as quickly as you can. Then, give yourself and the child time to move past the incident: *OK, that misstep is over now. What was going on with Sara? What do I need to change, reteach, or revisit for her future success?* After some time and space, return to the child and do some more proactive work.

If the Child Continues to Struggle

Sometimes, a child's misbehavior persists even after we've taught (and retaught) the expectations and responded effectively in the moment. Here are some other strategies to try when that happens:

Plan individual accommodations and arrangements

Some students need individual supports to help them break old habits or develop new ones. Students who tend to blurt out comments might respond to a private signal or reminder. Those who struggle to pay attention or find school stressful may benefit from having scheduled breaks or using "break request cards" that they can give the teacher when they need a few minutes to themselves. Look for ways to change, adapt, or modify expectations so that every student can succeed.

Hold class discussions

If, despite your proactive work, many children in your class are still having difficulties with the same issue, you may want to invite the whole class's input about what's going on and what needs to change. Here are some tips to ensure that these class discussions are effective:

- ***Start on a positive note.*** For instance, have students reflect on what the class has been doing well in following the class rules.
- ***Succinctly and matter-of-factly state the reason for the discussion.*** To avoid lecturing, blaming, or pleading with students, give a brief description of what you've noticed. For example: "We're meeting today to talk about some things I've noticed at quiet time and math. Sometimes I see and hear students making silly jokes or giggling long after a joke is over."
- ***Refer to the class rules.*** Let students know why the behavior is problematic by reminding them of its impact on their learning goals. Tie those goals to the class rules. For example: "When we are too silly during learning times, we're not living up to our classroom agreement to 'stay focused and do our best work.'"
- ***Use open-ended questions to explore students' ideas.*** When you invite students' input, you may gain greater insight into the problem and hear new ideas for solutions. Also, students may be

more invested in trying out these solutions if they feel they've been heard. You might ask, "How could we help each other if someone is still giggling when it's time to refocus?" or "What do you think could help us at quiet time or math?"

- ***Follow up on the discussion.*** One discussion may not be sufficient to address an ongoing issue. Keep reinforcing students' efforts and successes, and have them reflect on what's working, what's not, and what to do about lingering problems.

Use problem-solving conferences

A problem-solving conference is a way to get students more invested in changing their own behaviors. It's a private, one-on-one conversation in which the teacher and student work together to figure out what may be causing the behavior to continue, and then brainstorm and choose strategies to address it.

Teachers can hold these conferences as a ten- to fifteen-minute meeting with the student before or after school, at a private lunch, or while a colleague supervises the rest of the class. The teacher plans the conference beforehand, but also leaves ample room for student input.

- ***Start on a positive note.*** Begin the conversation by saying something positive about the student, such as by noting a recent accomplishment or some progress you've noticed.
- ***Name the problem and the need to solve it.*** Briefly describe the behavior: "I've noticed you often interrupt people during our discussions." Then, invite the student's input—"What have you noticed?"—before moving on to why the behavior is problematic, referencing the class rules and the behavior's effects on the student and others. For example: "When you interrupt, you're not following our rules to take care of our learning and each other. You miss key information and distract others." Last, confirm with him that he wants to work on the issue together.

- ***Examine possible reasons for the problem.*** Once the student agrees to work on the problem, talk about what may be causing it. It's helpful to come to the conference with two or three ideas of your own, but also invite the student to offer his own ideas. For example: "Could it be that you're so eager to participate that it makes it hard to wait until others are done speaking?" or "Some students jump in to talk because they want to show everyone they have really good ideas. Does that sound like what's going on for you?"
- ***Generate ideas for solutions.*** In advance, think of possible strategies to share at the conference, but be ready to adjust them based on the reasons identified for the behavior. Encourage the student to suggest strategies, too.
- ***Choose one strategy to try.*** Agree on a strategy to try and how you both will know if it's working. Set a date to meet again.

Consider an individual written agreement

Individual written agreements are designed to give a child highly structured, intense support to break a nonproductive habit and move toward positive behavior. The teacher and student agree on a behavior goal, a way to document her success in meeting it, and, if appropriate, a reward for meeting it.

Because these agreements can take up a significant amount of your time and often rely on extrinsic motivators, use them sparingly and only after trying other strategies. Here are some guidelines for using these agreements effectively:

- ***Set a specific goal.*** Establish a concrete and measurable goal for the student. For example: "Andrea will keep hands and feet to herself." Aim for a reasonable rate of success, such as seventy-five to eighty percent of the time, not perfection.
- ***Have a visible tracking method.*** Keep track of the incremental progress the child makes. For instance, keep track of how she does at given periods of the day or after certain time intervals. Every time the child meets the goal for that interval, give a visible reinforcement

and a verbal one. For instance, you might check off a box on a chart or add a Popsicle stick to a cup as you tell her what you noticed.

- ***Offer frequent feedback.*** Regular verbal reinforcement is important for this strategy to work effectively. The child needs to frequently hear that she's making progress toward her goal, rather than having to wait until the end of a day or the week. Such frequent positive feedback sustains a child and gives her hope that she can improve.

- ***Use a nontangible reward.*** When you set up the agreement, decide whether and how frequently the child will receive a reward for meeting the goal. Often children don't need a reward because the frequent teacher feedback and visible tracking of progress is motivating enough. Get to know your student well enough to judge what will motivate her.

  If you think a reward is needed, avoid offering something tangible, such as a toy or snack. Instead, offer an activity that would be special to the child, such as additional computer time or assisting a favorite teacher.

  One note of caution: Any extrinsic reward, even a nontangible one, can decrease a student's self-motivation if used for too long. Students eventually view the reward, rather than their and their classmates' productive learning, as the reason for positive behavior.

For in-depth guidance on problem-solving conferences and individual written agreements, see *Solving Thorny Behavior Problems: How Teachers and Students Can Work Together* by Caltha Crowe (Northeast Foundation for Children, 2009) and www.responsiveclassroom.org for free articles and more.

Seek help when you need it

Many teachers feel that it's a personal weakness to ask for help from colleagues about a student's behavior. In reality, collaborating with others is often a critical step in figuring out what the student needs and how best to help. Sources of help include other teachers, the special education team, school counselors, social workers, and administrators.

How to Communicate Respectfully With Parents About Behavior Challenges

Communicating with parents★ about a child's misbehavior is an important step to take to fully address the behavior and help the child learn how to meet expectations and be successful in school. Parents not only deserve to know how their child is doing in school, but they can be invaluable in helping to solve behavior issues if we bring them in on the problems.

★About the Term "Parent"

Many children are being raised by grandparents, siblings, aunts and uncles, foster families, and other caregivers. All of these individuals are to be honored for devoting their time, attention, and love to raising children.

In this book, for ease of reading, the term "parent" is used to represent all the caregivers involved in a child's life.

Let parents know you like their child

It can be very difficult for parents to trust a teacher's judgment about problems that arise if the teacher has never expressed genuine appreciation for their child. On the other hand, when parents know the teacher cares about and likes their child, they'll usually be more open to what the teacher has to say.

Make sure parents hear some positives, not just challenges

Many parents dread phone calls, notes, and emails from teachers. That's because these messages typically only mean one thing—bad news. You can remove this dread by regularly contacting parents to report that you've noticed their child's achievements and progress—a kind comment she made to a classmate or a strong effort on a difficult assignment. Parents will also be much more willing to hear what you have to say about their child's challenges if you share the positives with them on a regular basis.

Contact parents early on

Once you realize a child is beginning to struggle with a given behavior, go ahead and address the issue with parents even if it seems fairly minor. Tell parents what you've noticed and what strategies you're working on with the child. If you wait until the issue becomes a big one, parents may wonder why they are just now hearing about the problem.

Stick to "just the facts"

Avoid labeling or judging the child's behavior. Using loaded words will most likely result in parents' protective instincts rising up, making it harder for them to accept what you have to say. Be as specific and as objective as you can in describing what you've noticed. When you stick to the facts and paint a clear picture of what's going on, parents are much more likely to acknowledge their child's behavior and why it's problematic. Also, try to put yourself in their shoes and listen to your words from their perspective.

Talking With Parents Respectfully

Instead of this	Try this
"Alexa never listens and is rude."	"Alexa interrupts me and her classmates several times a day."
"Jonah has a real problem working with a partner."	"I've noticed that at math time, Jonah often keeps talking with the person next to him. Sometimes, that talking turns physical as Jonah pokes the person repeatedly."

Explain how the behavior hurts the child

Once you explain the facts, summarize why the behavior is problematic for the child. For example: "I worry that when Alexa interrupts, she doesn't hear important information. I'm also concerned that if she keeps interrupting her classmates, they may become reluctant to be her partner." When you explain to parents how their child's misbehavior might be harming her learning or social development, they're usually more invested in hearing what you have to say.

Be clear about the purpose of your communication

Know why you're sharing information about misbehavior with parents. Without that clarity, it can be easy for parents to feel that you're "dumping" a problem on them, blaming them, or leaving it up to them to find the solution. Here are some different reasons for sharing information:

- ***As an "FYI."*** Most often, the purpose of your communication will be to let parents know that their child is encountering difficulties and how you and the school are supporting him. Describe the strategies you've tried and how well they've worked. For example, you might start by saying, "I'd like to share with you the new strategies I'm working on with Eddie," and by letting parents know that you'll keep them posted; doing so makes it clear that you don't expect them to solve the problem.
- ***To gain new information.*** Parents often have insights that can help you better support their child at school. For instance, if a child was previously attentive during instructional times, but now she's making jokes or struggling to stay focused, her parents may be able to shed light on what might be affecting her.

➤ ***To seek help.*** Sometimes, you may want to enlist parents' help with an issue. For instance, you and the parents might decide to collaborate to help their child improve his organizational skills. Together, you might agree that you'll make sure the child brings his homework folder home every day, and that the parents will make sure homework and other papers make it into the folder, which then goes into their child's backpack every morning. Before asking for help, however, consider whether parents can realistically support what you're trying to do at school.

A Science and an Art

This chapter provided an overview of the *Responsive Classroom* approach to the science and art of discipline and classroom management. In the next chapters, you'll learn how to apply these strategies to many common misbehaviors. As you learn, study, and practice, you'll develop expertise—and get better and better at helping children maintain the positive behaviors that allow them to learn at their best.

A Summary of the *Responsive Classroom* Approach to Discipline

Proactive Strategies—How to Promote Positive Behavior

- Ensure basic needs are being met
- Build a safe, caring community
- Address social-emotional needs
- Plan engaging learning experiences and provide academic support as needed
- Establish clear expectations
- Create and display class rules
- Teach the rules and expectations
- Teach basic routines and procedures
- Use positive teacher language to set students up for success:
  - Give positive reminders
  - Reinforce students' progress

Reactive Strategies—How to Respond Effectively in the Moment

- Use nonverbal cues
- Move closer to the child (proximity)
- Use positive teacher language:
  - Remind children just as they're about to go off track
  - Redirect them if they've already gone off track
- Use logical consequences:
  - Loss of privilege
  - Reparation ("You break it, you fix it")
  - Positive time-out
- Tips for success:
  - Use a calm and respectful tone
  - Respond early to misbehavior
  - Don't take behavior personally
  - Maintain "clean slates" for all children
  - Continue using the proactive strategies

If the Child Continues to Struggle

- Plan individual accommodations and arrangements
- Use problem-solving conferences
- Consider individual written agreements
- Ask colleagues for help

Communicating With Parents

- Make sure parents know you like the child
- Tell parents some positives, not just the challenges
- Focus on "just the facts"
- Explain how the behavior hurts the child's learning
- Be clear about the purpose of your communication
- Keep your cool and maintain a professional demeanor at all times

1

Listening and Attention Challenges

Listening and Attention Challenges

Helping Children Listen and Pay Attention

Some complaints I hear frequently from teachers—*"Too much talking!" "They won't listen!" "No one is paying attention!"*—are ones I keenly felt when I first started teaching. Too often, while we teach, students excitedly chat away as if we aren't even there.

In today's multitasking world, everyone struggles with staying focused, and school is no different. Children regularly interrupt teachers and classmates, engage in frequent side conversations during lessons, or have trouble holding

their attention for more than a few minutes. Sometimes children listen closely during engaging discussions, but then lose focus when it's time to receive directions and get started on their work.

When children struggle with listening, it isn't just frustrating to teachers, it also detracts from the children's learning. Fortunately, you can help your students develop the skills they need to listen and focus, and redirect them when their attention lags. In this chapter, you'll learn why children struggle to listen, strategies for helping children improve their listening, how to respond when they do forget to listen (because they will forget, just as we adults do!), and how to talk effectively with parents of children who struggle with listening.

Why Is Listening Hard for Children?

Children struggle to listen for many of the same reasons adults do—they're tired, hungry, or thirsty; they're bored, distracted, or stressed; or they lack the skills. Of course, the exact reasons vary from child to child and situation to situation. Here are some common reasons for children's listening struggles.

Unmet physical needs

It takes a lot of energy to maintain self-control, which is essential for listening. So it's hard for children to focus when they're hungry, thirsty, or tired, or when they've been sitting still for a long time. Think about your listening abilities during a staff meeting after a long day of teaching. Consider how diminished your abilities are if you missed lunch. The same applies to children: To do their best listening, they need to be energized with enough sleep, enough to eat and drink, and frequent opportunities to move.

Looking for fun

Remember that having fun is a basic human need. If a lesson doesn't engage children or seems irrelevant to their lives, they'll look for other ways to entertain themselves. Some children may daydream; others may try to engage classmates in silly conversations or play. While we cannot and should not have to make every moment of school fun and exciting, the more we design lessons that are developmentally appropriate and interesting to students, the more likely they will listen and attend.

Wanting to belong and feel significant

Children may chat during lessons, engage in side conversations, pass around notes, or make a funny face at a neighbor simply to feel connected to classmates. For these children, ignoring the lesson has little to do with us or the lesson. Instead, it has to do with their desire to get to know and be known by others. Even children who ordinarily listen can have a hard time resisting this desire if their classmates start to chat or fool around.

Weak listening skills

Some children lack the skills to listen for an extended period of time. Maybe no one has ever explicitly taught these children how to listen, or they haven't yet had enough practice. Other children may have developed habits that work against them at school—daydreaming, tuning out adults, multitasking, or interrupting. Whatever the reason, they now need to build up their listening skills for success in school.

Listening struggles and child development

A child's attention skills typically develop over time, but this growth is not always smooth. At certain stages of childhood, it's common to see developmental characteristics that may affect a child's ability to focus and listen.

Some Child Development Characteristics Related to Listening Struggles		
Grade	**Characteristic**	**Influence on listening**
Kindergarten (ages 4–6)	• Need to move regularly • Learn best through concrete experiences • Tend to verbalize as they think	• Unable to sit for long stretches in whole-group settings • Need to talk more to process what they're learning • Need hands-on activities to break up "sit-and-listen" times
1st (ages 5–7)	• Tire easily • Need to move a lot • Very social; concerned with social issues • Very verbal; like to explain things	• Need more chances to move • More concerned with social issues than academics • Need to process what they're learning by talking
3rd (ages 7–9)	• Very social; concerned with social issues • Like to talk; full of ideas • Experiencing a growth spurt; need physical movement	• Could use more time to connect with friends, even around academics • Need more chances to talk to process learning • Need more chances to move
5th (ages 9–11)	• Experiencing large muscle growth spurt; need physical movement • Very social • Expressive; talkative	• May need more frequent opportunities to stretch, change position, and be active • Need more time with friends • May need more time to talk or to verbally process learning

Of course, children in any grade may have listening or focusing challenges. However, if you teach the grades represented in the chart, think especially carefully about how to address these issues proactively. It may take children time to develop listening skills, but when you convey confidence that they can improve, along with patiently providing instruction, practice, and coaching, they do succeed!

Building Up the Listening Muscles

Proactive Steps to Promote Listening

The goal of proactive work in this area is to help children learn listening skills that will help them be successful at school and beyond. As with any muscle, children develop their listening and attention muscles over time, not overnight. It's important to be empathetic, and look for progress, not perfection.

Here are some proactive steps to take to help students hone their listening skills.

TEACHING TIP

Listening Skills

Scaffold—start small, requiring attentive listening for a short period of time, and then build up.

Be explicit about what listening looks and sounds like (eyes on speaker, hands still, mouth quiet, etc.).

Teach specific conversation skills, such as turn-taking, raising hands, respectfully agreeing and disagreeing, and being succinct.

Give children chances to practice listening in fun ways—for example, through games such as Simon Says or by challenging them to listen for and recall events from a story.

Explicitly teach what listening looks, sounds, and feels like

My mentor Paula Denton, whose experience teaching children and adults spans over thirty years, used a phrase that resonated for my students and me: "solid gold attention." When children give their focused attention, the positive feelings in the room are palpable and their readiness to learn is noticeable. Yet, we can't assume that children know how to give that sort of undivided attention. School expectations for listening may also be different from those at home.

First, get a sense of your students' needs and abilities, and then adjust your teaching accordingly. Interactive Modeling (see pages 24–25) is an effective way to teach listening skills, including how to sit, where eyes should go, where hands should be, how to show engagement, and so on. If possible, collaborate with special area teachers and others who work with your students so that you all convey consistent expectations for listening and teach the same skills.

Make listening worthwhile for students

The more engaging lessons are, the more intently students will listen. One key is to plan lessons that build on students' interests, strengths, and developmental needs and abilities. For instance, the squirmy, chatty kindergartners I taught became incredibly focused the minute read-aloud began. So I learned to make all instruction more like that time of day. I used stories and real-life events to make math come alive. During writing workshop, I started writing about my own dog's adventures to make mini-lessons and interactive writing lessons more intriguing for students.

In a fifth grade class I visited, students engaged in a lively debate about an issue that truly captivated their attention—bullying. On another day, this class played a game focused on the statement "Children should have less homework." Students were assigned the "pro" side or "con" side. Then, they had to defend their position with as many reasons as possible.

All these debates and discussions required the students to practice their listening skills. What topics and activities grab your students' attention? The time you spend thinking about how to gain students' interest (and hold it) will pay off in terms of children's listening and focus.

Keep direct instruction time brief

Most of us can sit and listen for only a fairly short period of time. Keep in mind your students' ages and abilities as you plan how long to talk. Start with relatively short presentations and lengthen them gradually as your students develop more stamina for focused listening.

Give children chances to move around

As we teach, we usually move around, but it's easy to forget that children are not always doing the same. So break up your direct teaching with a movement break or a change in location. Have them stand up for a few minutes to discuss something interesting with partners. Or have students express their opinion on an issue through a Four Corners activity (with each corner representing a different response).

Give children options for participating in discussions

Establish nonverbal signals to show agreement, disagreement, or a connection to what someone is saying (thumbs up, thumbs down, etc.), so they're more likely to stay tuned in and feel part of the group while they listen. The same happens when students have a chance to verbally participate through a choral response or a repeated refrain.

Change your tone, face, and body language as needed

Because much of what we communicate comes through our nonverbal cues, use your posture, facial expression, and tone of voice to capture children's interest. For instance, when teaching students about an historical event, you might use a low and soft voice, then gradually become louder and more animated as you reach the high point of the event. As you move toward the conclusion of the lesson, you could slow down and again speak more softly.

Here are more tips for keeping students tuned in to you:

- ***Have a confident, open posture.*** For example, smile and make eye contact with children when they speak. This invites students to trust and listen to you.
- ***Show excitement when warranted.*** I recently watched a fourth grade teacher do a read-aloud. Her students were captivated as she used different voices for each character and read with enthusiasm.
- ***Use correct intonation.*** When we ask questions, our tone should go up, ending on a high note. When giving directions, our tone should indicate a clear statement, not a question or request. Match your tone to your words, so students clearly understand what you want them to do.
- ***Be conscious of your facial expressions.*** If we look bored or distracted when we present information, the message we send is "Let's just get through this" and students will respond in kind. When, instead, our faces show enjoyment, excitement, or even confusion when appropriate, students will be more likely to match our emotions and respond with greater focus.

- ***Make effective eye contact.*** If you watch a master teacher, one of the first things you'll notice is how effectively she uses her eyes to communicate with students. To students paying attention, she smiles and looks briefly at them. To those who look upset or confused, she responds with a sympathetic or a questioning look. To a student who's about to go off track, her eyes convey that focus is needed.
- ***Build in pauses to give children time to think.*** Students need time to process what they're hearing. Include natural pauses or add in stopping points to give students reflection time (count in your head or use the second hand on a clock if you need to).

Build in time for students to talk productively with classmates

Students need to feel a sense of connectedness with each other throughout the day. Rather than fight this need, harness it for learning. For example, address some content through conversations between students. Give them a chance to turn and talk with a partner about an intriguing question you've raised. When students work independently, allow for brief, quiet conversations. Teach them how to check in with those near them, ask a question, and share in meaningful ways.

Be the model for focused listening and quiet attention

Students often learn by copying us. When you're with students, parents, and colleagues, demonstrate the same kind of listening skills you're trying to instill in your students. No matter who's talking, show that you're listening intently.

Help children attend to directions

Listening to directions can be challenging for children because most don't naturally find that kind of information engaging. However, several strategies can help you set students up for success in this area:

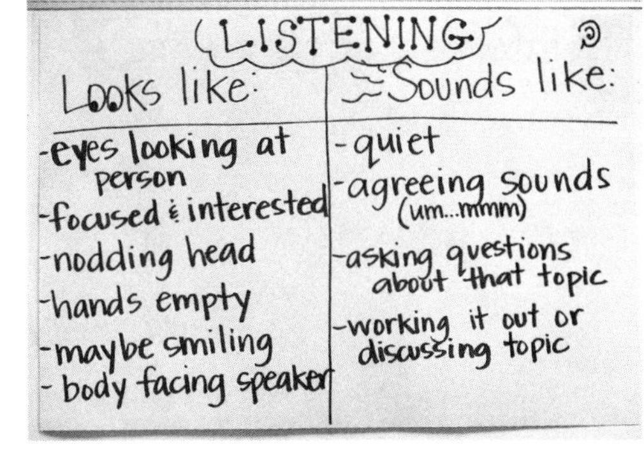

- ***Say directions once.*** Students will listen more carefully if they know you won't repeat yourself.

- ***Have students repeat directions back.*** Especially for more complicated or multistep directions, have students recap directions with a partner or randomly call on students to repeat key steps for the whole group.

- ***Post written directions.*** This keeps you from having to repeat instructions, and it supports students who struggle to remember multistep directions.

- ***Direct students to classmates for help.*** If students didn't hear or can't remember the directions, have them rely on each other, not you. This strengthens their interdependence and sense of community.

Arrange the classroom to support listening

In the area where you do direct instruction, try to give children enough space to be comfortable. When students feel crammed in, they're more prone to distractions.

Also, experiment with having only a few essential visual displays. When classrooms are crowded with displays, students can get overwhelmed and distracted. And think about where students sit. Consider assigning and regularly reassigning seats in the whole group. This will prevent children from always sitting next to those with whom they're tempted to chat while enabling them to interact with a variety of classmates.

For more on setting up your classroom to support learning, see *Classroom Spaces That Work* by Marlynn K. Clayton (Northeast Foundation for Children, 2001), *What Every Teacher Needs to Know,* K–5 series by Margaret Berry Wilson and Mike Anderson (Northeast Foundation for Children, 2010–2011), and www.responsiveclassroom.org for free articles and more.

Reinforce students' efforts at listening

To encourage children's growth in focusing and listening, point out what they're doing well—and why that matters for their learning.

Reinforcing Language in Action	
If a situation like this happens	**Try this**
Most students listen, focus, and engage with material during a whole-class presentation.	"That was a productive conversation. We learned so much because you were all focused, participating, and listening to each other. Now it's time to apply what we discussed."
All students, many of whom have previously struggled with side conversations, keep their focus on you and other speakers.	"You all listened respectfully! Your bodies were leaning forward slightly, your eyes were on the speaker, and you resisted the urge to chat with your neighbors."
Several students have been struggling to wait until speakers finish before raising their hands. During today's discussion, you notice that they follow that expectation for the first few minutes.	"So far, everyone has remembered to listen until the speaker has finished before raising a hand to have a turn. We've been working on that rule and you're definitely making progress."
A child who often blurts out answers raises her hand three times during a class discussion.	*(Privately)* "Lisbeth, you remembered our rule about raising hands during today's discussion. That helps make sure only one person is talking at a time, so everyone can listen better. What's helping you remember?"

Refocusing Students' Attention

How to Respond Effectively in the Moment

Even if you proactively teach students listening skills and expectations—and reteach and reinforce those regularly—there will be times when they don't meet expectations. Remember, listening is a skill that will take children time and practice to build up. So, be patient. Trust that they'll improve even as you respond decisively to the inevitable lapses.

Be clear, respectful, and not punitive in responding to children's lapses. Your goal is to quickly shift the child's focus back to learning and keep the rest of the class learning as well. Here are some tips for doing that.

Respond quickly

It's best to respond to a student as soon as you see any sign that he's getting off track with listening or focus. When, for instance, you quickly redirect a student just as he's about to chat with a neighbor, you give him a better chance to refocus. If, instead, you wait until he's in the middle of a conversation, it will take much more of an effort to get him—and now his classmate—back on track. Similarly, if you stop the first student who calls out, other students are less likely to follow.

Respond consistently

No matter if a student talks to a neighbor, calls out when someone else is speaking, or shows signs of distraction, respond the same way. If you let some side conversations go on or engage with a student who calls out, you send mixed messages: "It's OK to chat sometimes" or "You don't have to raise your hand all the time."

Consistency also means that you respond to whomever is not listening or focusing. If you single out some students but not others, a sense of unfairness can divide the class and invite further testing. Consistent, respectful responses hold all children accountable for giving their attention to the speaker.

Keep the learning going

What often makes teaching challenging is the constant monitoring that's required—of individual students and of the class as a whole, and all at the same time! When a child isn't listening, you need to respond to her specific misstep, yet still keep your focus on the rest of your class. If you devote too much attention to her, you may lose everyone else. So respond with a quick strategy from below without breaking the pace or theme of your lesson.

Remind, redirect, and use proximity

Three effective strategies you can use to shift students' attention back to the lesson are giving reminders, giving redirections, and using proximity (moving closer to the child). The table that follows gives you some ideas for how to use the strategies.

Reminding, Redirecting, and Using Proximity

If a situation like this happens	Try this
Lots of children start chattering at once while you're talking.	• **Remind (nonverbal):** Stop talking and use your signal for quiet attention. • **Redirect and remind (verbal):** "Freeze. Voices off; eyes on me. Everyone take a few deep breaths." Let students be silent together for thirty seconds. Then, give a quick reminder of the expectations and restart: "This time, while I'm talking, everyone needs to look at me and listen, the way we practiced."
Sarah and Emilio start having a side conversation.	• **Use proximity:** Move closer to the two students. • **Redirect:** "Sarah and Emilio, eyes up here."

If a situation like this happens	Try this
Erika calls out an answer without raising her hand (or using another designated signal).	• **Remind (nonverbal):** Shake your head to show Erika that you will not call on her. Then, raise your hand to remind her of the rules. • **Redirect:** "Erika, try again. Show me the way we practiced for getting called on."
Devon begins to fidget, wiggle, or show other visible signs of struggling with attention.	• **Use proximity:** Move closer to Devon as you keep speaking and make eye contact with him. • **Redirect the individual student:** "Devon, go back to my counter and grab the Popsicle sticks I use to call on people." (This helps the child move and use up some energy.) • **Redirect the class:** One student's struggles may be a warning sign that others are also struggling or will be soon. Have all students do a partner chat. Then check in with Devon to see what he needs.

Use logical consequences if needed

Sometimes, your instincts may tell you that for this particular child's failure to listen in this particular situation, you should use a logical consequence as the quickest way to get the child back on track. At other times, you might have tried reminding, redirecting, or using proximity, but it hasn't stopped the problem behavior. In these situations, logical consequences would also be appropriate as shown in the table that follows.

Logical Consequences in Action	
If a situation like this happens	**Try this**
Sarah and Emilio continue having a side conversation.	• **Loss of privilege:** Move one student: "Emilio, come sit beside me." • **Time-out:** "Sarah, Emilio, go to our take-a-break spots."
Erika calls out answers without raising her hand.	• **Time-out:** "Erika, take a time-out."
Manami continues to flip her hair back and forth over her face during instruction.	• **Time-out:** "Manami, time-out."
In a math lesson, you direct students to pause and take their hands off the manipulatives as you give the next set of directions. Estefan begins to build with his manipulatives.	• **Loss of privilege:** "Estefan, come sit in front of me during directions." • **Loss of privilege:** "Estefan, I'm going to hold onto your pattern blocks so that you can hear the directions."

To learn more about logical consequences, see pages 32–35.

In those moments when children are struggling with listening, your responses remind children of the expectations and their responsibilities. But students will also need you to continue teaching the skills of listening through the proactive strategies discussed previously on pages 51–56. Remember that the proactive and in-the-moment steps work best when used in concert.

If a Child Continues to Struggle With Listening

Sometimes listening challenges persist despite your concerted uses of proactive and in-the-moment steps. When this occurs, try some of these additional strategies.

Invite the student's input

Children often have more insight into their behaviors and strategies for dealing with them than we realize. I once taught a student whom I had been keeping close to me as a strategy for improving his listening. He told me that he found it distracting to be in the front because he was wondering what everyone behind him was doing. I moved him and, sure enough, that helped.

Use a problem-solving conference to talk privately with your student. The goal is to pinpoint why listening is hard for her and explore strategies that might help. Often, just the process of including the child in working on the problem can help her be more invested in solving it.

To prepare for the conference, think about:

- ***What to say*** to get the conference started on a positive note.
- ***How to state the problem*** in concrete terms the child will understand. For example: "When we are on the rug, you play with your shoes, talk to the person next to you, and often don't hear what I say."
- ***Possible causes of the problem.*** If the child is at a loss as to what's causing her listening struggles, name some possible reasons and see if the child thinks any ring true. Also, be open to the child's ideas.
- ***Strategies that may help,*** such as you giving the child a secret signal when she needs to refocus her attention, or the child giving you a card when she needs a break from listening. Remember to also encourage the child to share some strategies of her own.

Seek help from colleagues

If you're unsure what to do next or if the problem behavior seems firmly entrenched, seek help from another teacher, a school counselor, or a learning specialist. Colleagues who are also teaching the child or have taught her in the past may have ideas you can try. Or, you could invite a colleague to come observe the child in action and see if she notices issues you've missed or can suggest strategies you had not considered.

Use an individual written agreement

If you have tried several strategies unsuccessfully and addressed (or ruled out) any learning or other issues that may be interfering with a child's ability to listen, consider an individual written agreement. An individual written agreement gives the child specific behavior goals to accomplish and frequent feedback about whether he's meeting those goals. By breaking the task of listening down into specific behaviors—and by giving the child positive feedback—these agreements can provide the extra support that some children need to succeed with listening.

Here's how such an agreement might look and sound:

- ***Set a clearly defined goal.*** For example: "Andrew will stay in his spot, keep his eyes on the speaker, and raise his hand to make any comments."
- ***Use a reasonable standard for success*** in meeting the goal. For example: "Andrew will be successful eighty percent of the time."
- ***Have a way to track success*** that's easy for the student to see and understand—check marks on a chart or craft sticks in a jar, for instance.
- ***Have a nontangible reward*** for meeting the goal. For example: "If Andrew meets the goal, he can go help the kindergarten teacher with end-of-the-day tasks for ten minutes."

How to Talk With Parents About Listening Struggles

For most parents, it's difficult to hear that their child has listening or focusing challenges. Some may immediately worry about attention deficit disorder. Others may feel that their parenting style or cultural background is at issue. And many parents may simply feel powerless to do anything about how their child listens at school.

These are factors to keep in mind when talking with parents about their child's struggles. The key is to note your observations objectively. Steer clear of labeling the child, suggesting a diagnosis, or providing medical-related advice. Instead, stick to describing what you have noticed at school. Share all the proactive strategies you're using to foster listening.

Remember also to note the successes you observe. Parents will be more receptive to what you say if they realize that you appreciate their child, are working to help her with all the complexities of listening, and believe that she can succeed. As always, be open to what families share with you.

Communicating With Parents

Instead of	Try
Using general language • "Sean can't seem to listen or pay attention. No matter what we're doing, he seems off in another world."	**Giving specific details** • "At times in our whole-group discussions, Sean plays with his shoes and doesn't look at the person speaking. At other times, he talks when others are talking."
Expressing defeat • "Lucinda is such a chatterbox. She can't stop talking no matter who sits next to her."	**Naming the proactive steps you're taking** • "Each lesson, I make sure all students have a chance to turn and talk with a neighbor, and I don't expect total silence during work times. I've also been working with Lucinda to help her channel her outgoing nature in productive ways."

CONTINUED ON PAGE 64

Instead of	Try
Being judgmental • "Aisha bothers her classmates with her talking and fidgeting. No one wants to sit near her."	**Describing objectively** • "Sometimes Aisha doesn't listen to directions and then interrupts her classmates to see what she missed. Other times, she distracts them when they're working and they get frustrated with her. This is what I'm working with Aisha on . . ."
Shifting responsibility to the parent • "I need you to talk with Bryan about listening and how important it is at school."	**Being partners** • "I would like to share with you some strategies I'm using to help Bryan develop stronger listening skills. If you have ideas, I'd like to hear those, too."

Some parents may have been worrying about their child's abilities to listen and focus long before you raise the issue, so when you do, they may be relieved and looking for help. If parents seek advice, here are some general tips you may want to offer them:

- ***Set up work times*** in ways that support attention. Pick a consistent time of day and a distraction-free area for homework and similar projects. Breaking the work up can help. For instance, set a goal for the child of doing two problems in the next five minutes. When she does that, give reinforcing feedback: "You did it. You focused on two problems and completed them." Then, set a goal for the next five minutes and so on.
- ***Focus on listening skills*** that are important for school success. Taking turns, not interrupting, and showing interest are just three such skills. One simple way to help a child practice these skills is to have family members take turns talking about their day during a shared meal.
- ***Reinforce positive attention and listening.*** Watch for times when the child is carefully listening, following directions, and being attentive. Let her know that her behavior was noticed. For example, say, "I noticed that you waited to talk until I finished." This motivates the child to keep up similar behavior in the future.

Closing Thoughts

As you help children develop their abilities to focus and listen, remember to have empathy for their struggles. You can hold them to high (and reasonable) expectations while keeping in mind that listening and focusing are challenging for everyone, especially in today's fast-paced world. Stay patient, look for signs of progress, and reinforce them. After all, you're helping children build up some of the most important "muscles" they'll ever need—their listening muscles!

Key Points

Use proactive strategies, such as modeling what listening looks and sounds like, to help children improve their focusing and listening skills.

Respond at the first sign a child is not listening. Effective strategies include redirecting, reminding, and using proximity.

Avoid labeling, diagnosing, or suggesting treatment when communicating with parents about a child's struggles with listening. Instead, describe the child's specific behavior in a matter-of-fact way, let parents know what you've tried, and be open to their ideas.

2

Teasing

Teasing

Teaching Children How to Respect Everyone

These were the words, chanted as students returned from PE one day, that set off my internal teacher alarm: *"Rachel and Jackson are boyfriend and girlfriend! They L-O-V-E each other."*

My previously kind second graders were experimenting with teasing each other about boy-girl friendships. This kind of "love teasing" didn't happen every year, but when it did, it typically occurred in the spring.

That spring, if a boy and girl played together at recess or were work partners, their classmates would tease them or point and giggle. This teasing, innocent in intent, still hurt. I knew that if I didn't act quickly, some boys and girls

might stop playing together. Others might worry about coming to school; a few might get angry and lash back. To air out the effects of these taunts and hold students accountable for their words, I gathered them for a class discussion.

"I've heard people saying that some children in our class are boyfriend and girlfriend. That makes people feel uncomfortable. It can even make people not want to be friends anymore. When we say things that hurt others, it breaks our class rule 'Take care of each other.' Today, I want us to brainstorm ideas about what we can do to take better care of each other."

After a thoughtful discussion, the students came up with a list of strategies, including telling the person to stop or telling me if teasing happened. In the weeks ahead, we frequently returned to the list and I checked in at the first sign that the problem was recurring.

Although we wish it weren't so, the truth is that as children develop, they sometimes tease each other, call names, and say other unkind things. They do so for many reasons, related to their social-emotional needs, their efforts to figure out the line between humor and meanness, and their still-developing social skills, especially empathy.

Clearly, teasing can be innocent and playful, and we often find some instances of it hilarious. My students loved kidding me about my frequent, but unsuccessful, attempts to give up diet soda, laughed with each other when, as often occurred, someone forgot to put their bathroom card back ("Are you still in there?"), or looked over with affection at Marissa when we reread a poem that she had said "made my head spin."

As teachers, however, we need to keep an eye on these attempts at playful, relational humor because it's easy for them to cross the line into meanness. Children need our guidance to know what kinds of joking and teasing are OK and what kinds are not, and why. It was fine for my students to joke with me about my diet soda habit because I had raised the issue, but it would not be OK to tease others about their lunch. Two friends might joke with each other about how clumsy they were on the stairs, but calling someone "clumsy" out of the blue crosses the line.

We can't assume that children will figure out where that line is on their own. We need to teach them. We need to proactively show them how to be respectful and have fun with classmates. And when children, despite our proactive teaching, say words that have the potential to hurt others, we have another golden opportunity to teach.

Through our responses, we can help children become thoughtful about what they say and how they say it, and we can help our classroom communities feel safe to all. If, instead, we ignore mean comments or discount them as "just a joke," we send an entirely different message. Inadvertently, we may be encouraging students to use more harmful and extreme levels of teasing or other mean behavior.

In this chapter, you'll learn why children tease, how to teach children to be playful without being hurtful, practical ways to redirect students when they make mistakes and say mean words, and how to talk with parents about teasing.

Why Do Children Tease Each Other?

Children who tease, call names, and put others down are often trying to meet their needs for belonging, significance, and fun. Children may also tease and say unkind things because they lack certain social skills or because they're testing out behaviors.

The desire to belong

It may seem counterintuitive, but students may tease each other to fulfill their need for belonging. They may come to school having learned that teasing is a way to show affection. Or maybe that's how they've seen television characters treat friends. They may genuinely think they're being playful with the person they're teasing—and not recognize that their words actually hurt.

Sometimes children want to become closer friends with a classmate, but they're not sure how to approach that person. They tease to get that person's attention. Finally, children often tease because others are teasing. They'll join in to show and feel that they belong, too.

The need to feel powerful

Some children may gain a sense of significance and power through teasing. If classmates laugh when Ted makes a "funny" comment about someone else's appearance, Ted may suddenly feel a lot more important. The fear and hurt a child caused—to those he teased and to those who witnessed the teasing—can also reinforce these feelings. And, if the child begins to feel this power, he may continue the teasing or go even further with it.

Looking for fun

Frequently, children say they were just "having a little fun" or "playing around" with their teasing. They may even enjoy the reactions their teasing causes and feel silly and engaged.

A lack of social skills

Children may say unkind things or tease others because they lack certain social skills. For example, they may not know what to do when they meet someone new and thus say something unkind. They may not yet have the social skills of engaging in polite, respectful conversations and not grasp the harmful effects words can have.

Teasing and child development

Teasing occurs throughout the grade levels. However, it may be more common at certain developmental stages.

Some Child Development Characteristics Related to Teasing		
Grade	Characteristic	Influence on teasing
Kindergarten (ages 4–6)	• Often think out loud • Struggle to see issues from others' point of view	• Don't understand the difference between spoken words and internal thoughts • Can't yet fully understand the impact of words
1st (ages 5–7)	• Sometimes critical of others • Can be very competitive or "poor sports"	• May not yet fully understand impact of criticism • May get caught up in the moment and put others down during the course of a game or activity
4th (ages 8–10)	• Can be very critical of themselves and others • Can be very competitive • Often experimenting with humor (exaggeration, inside jokes, etc.)	• May temporarily feel better about themselves by putting others down • May not realize when a joke has crossed the line
6th (ages 10–12)	• Often moody and sensitive • Sometimes cruel and even physically aggressive • Often impulsive	• May want to boost flagging feelings of significance by putting others down • May speak quickly and not think about effects on others

If you teach one of the grade levels listed, be especially prepared for teasing and other mean uses of words. But these behaviors can and do happen in all grades. It's important to teach all children how to use words respectfully and to take care of each other.

Fewer Mean Words, More Kind Words

Proactive Steps to Promote Respectful Language

Preventing teasing, name-calling, and put-downs requires teaching children how to be kind and respectful to one another while still having fun. Establish clear expectations about appropriate language and then teach students how to meet those expectations.

Make sure class rules require respectful language

When you establish rules with students, make sure at least one rule supports respectful language. For example: "Be kind to each other." "Respect one another." "Take care of each other."

Teach what respectful language looks and sounds like

Of course, it's not enough to have a rule. For children to follow a rule about respecting others, you'll need to explicitly teach what it looks, sounds, and feels like in action.

Effective ways to do that are through morning meetings, Interactive Modeling, role-plays, and class discussions. At morning meetings, students can learn how to greet each other, have respectful conversations, and play games that are joyful for all. (For a list of morning meeting resources, see page 256.) You can do Interactive Modeling lessons or role-plays (see pages 24–25) on how to have an enjoyable, polite conversation at lunch; how to show appreciation for friends; and how to joke and have fun in nonhurtful ways.

Children's literature can also provide great opportunities to discuss situations in which characters engage in humor that's fun for all and those in which their joking is hurtful (see pages 252–255 for children's book suggestions).

Revisit the rule as necessary

Often, as students get more comfortable with one another, teasing increases. When this occurs, have a class discussion in which you revisit the rule that governs respectful language. For these discussions to be effective, follow these guidelines:

- ***Tell children not to name others*** or describe an incident in a way that lets everyone know whom they're discussing.
- ***Hold these discussions only for issues that are continuous*** and involve many children. Don't have a whole-class discussion in response to one particular incident. Instead, address it privately with the children involved.
- ***Make sure all voices are heard*** and that children work together toward a solution.
- ***If you suspect bullying*** or unequal power between the children involved, don't hold a class discussion. Instead, work individually with the child doing the bullying, following school protocols. Be sure to protect the child who was targeted from further meanness. Meanwhile, teach the whole class general lessons on mean behaviors so that everyone feels safe and can do their best learning. For more about bullying prevention, see *How to Bullyproof Your Classroom* by Caltha Crowe (Northeast Foundation for Children, 2012).

TEACHING TIP

Words Can't Be Taken Back

Young children often think they can take back hurtful words by saying a quick "I'm sorry." They need to learn that once words leave their mouths, they can't be taken back. To teach this lesson, try the Toothpaste Squeeze activity:

Tell students that when they say a hurtful word, it's like squeezing out toothpaste.

Go around the circle and let each student squirt a little toothpaste into a plastic bowl.

Go back around and challenge students to put the toothpaste back. They'll try but find that it's impossible.

Tell students that words work the same way: once out, we can't put them back.

If you have older students who need the same teaching, consider using children's books to discuss how characters felt in hurtful situations or talk about the effects of bullying incidents in the news.

Continue to build community

Throughout the year, keep fostering children's sense of togetherness by providing many opportunities for them to interact positively with every classmate. For example:

- ***Frequently play games that build community spirit*** and help children get to know each other, such as The Warm Wind Blows or Group Juggling. For resources on fun games and energizers, see page 258.
- ***Build in structures for students to share news*** and receive questions and comments from classmates.
- ***Teach children how to give meaningful compliments.*** Periodically have "compliment circles" during which each student offers and receives a compliment (assign names ahead of time).

Teach students about teasing's impact

As Stephen Wessler argues eloquently in his book *The Respectful School*, it's important for children to learn the difference between the impact of their words and their intent. To help children understand that their words can hurt even if that's not what they intended, use concrete examples such as incidents from children's books. Then, have students reflect on whether simply knowing the person "didn't mean to" would make their hurt go away. For a list of helpful children's books, see pages 252–255.

Students also need to learn that words can hurt not just the person teased, but anyone standing nearby. For example, when children use epithets such as "retarded," someone with a sibling who has developmental challenges may overhear. That bystander may then feel deeply hurt. Children need our help to learn about the damage words can cause and how to use words to care for, not harm, others.

Teach the difference between school speech and out-of-school speech

Outside of school, children often tease and call each other names in ways friendly and not so friendly. In one sixth grade classroom I visited, the teacher told me that outside of school, some of her female students regularly called each other the "b-word" as a sign of affection. Students can and should understand, however, that school expectations may differ from those outside the school.

Teach children what to do if they notice teasing

It's impossible for teachers to observe everything that occurs, but we can teach children what to do and empower them to act if they see or hear teasing. Teach and model how to:

- ***Be friendly.*** Talk about the difference a single act of kindness—such as a warm smile or asking, "Want to play with me?"—can make to someone being teased. Use Interactive Modeling, role-play, class discussions, and children's books to explore and bring this idea to life.
- ***Use physical proximity.*** Explain how moving closer to someone who is being teased often stops the teasing and helps him feel better (because he has an ally). Again, make this point visible for children through Interactive Modeling or role-play.
- ***Be assertive.*** Teach how to tell a classmate to stop teasing or remind her respectfully of class rules. Use Interactive Modeling or role-play to have students focus on the words and tone to use to be firm and respectful. For example, they might remind the classmate with "Classroom rules" or "School words" or prompt her with "Erase!" or "Do over!"

  A note of caution: It can be unhelpful if not dangerous for bystanders to confront a classmate whose teasing has crossed into bullying. Teach children that if a situation feels unsafe in any way, they should report the behavior to you or another adult.

➤ ***Report problems to adults.*** Teach when and how to report a problem. Let students know that if in doubt about whether words are hurtful, they should always tell an adult. To learn more about the differences between tattling and reporting, see Chapter 4.

Model what respect looks and sounds like

Just like most students, most teachers would never intentionally hurt a student's feelings. However, in our attempts to build relationships with students, we might use nicknames (calling a tall red-headed child "Big Red") or use sarcasm ("Did you wake up on the wrong side of the bed?"). Or we might laugh when we shouldn't.

TEACHING TIP

Being Respectful of Students' Names

Properly pronouncing and using children's names is another way we can model respect. If we regularly mispronounce a student's name or say it in a way that shows we find it strange, we send a message that it's OK for students to do the same.

If, instead, we take the time to learn how to say each child's name and then stick to that correct pronunciation, we reinforce the notion that everyone is valued. In addition:

- **Avoid nicknames** or making rhymes with students' names.
- **Use morning meetings,** group activities, and other times of day to help students learn each other's names and use them respectfully.
- **Teach students how to respond respectfully** if someone mispronounces their names. For example: "My name is actually pronounced ________. It's Filipino."

One year my assistant teacher proudly came in with a new haircut. A student looked up and said sympathetically, "Bad hair day, Ms. F?" I laughed and in so doing sent everyone the wrong message. Although neither the student nor I meant to hurt Ms. F's feelings, we did—and my students learned that making fun of someone was OK. It took a lot of effort to undo this unfortunate lesson!

So always be mindful of whether your actions match the expectations you have laid out for students. Avoid doing even a "little" teasing or name-calling, or laughing or smiling at teasing. Instead, show students what it looks like to have fun without hurting someone else's feelings.

Reinforce kindness and respect when you see them

Pay attention to students' efforts to be kind and respectful, and point these out when you notice them. The more you reinforce kind words and deeds, the more students will use them.

Reinforcing Language in Action	
For a situation like this	**Try this**
At lunch, you sit with a group of students who get along well but often tease in ways that can be hurtful. At this particular lunch, they're joking in ways that feel comfortable to all.	**To the group:** "That was a fun lunch! You made each other laugh and took care of each other at the same time."
A student self-corrects when he's about to call a buddy by a derogatory name they use outside of school.	**Privately:** "Jim, you stopped yourself from using a hurtful word. Self-correcting is a strategy we talked about and one way to follow our rule of speaking kindly to others."
A student tells you about how she witnessed her classmate making fun of a new classmate's backpack.	**Privately:** "Coming to tell me about this really takes care of our new classmate. I will take it from here."
A child has been working on not calling others names. Although he still sometimes makes mistakes, you have seen definite improvement.	**Privately:** "Todd, when you worked with Roberto, I noticed you encouraging him even when he made mistakes. I see the effort you're putting into using kinder language with your classmates."

Taming Teasing

How to Respond Effectively in the Moment

Proactive measures will help prevent a lot of teasing but won't eliminate it. As students try to figure out how to meet their needs in acceptable ways, they'll inevitably make mistakes. When they do, we need to respond respectfully and matter-of-factly, reinforcing our proactive teaching while giving the unequivocal message that teasing is not acceptable. Here are some tips:

Respond immediately

When we respond right away to students' mean words, we help those students and all those around them understand what respect requires. If we ignore mean words, thinking they'll go away, we instead communicate that this type of language is OK. Children may interpret our nonresponse as a go-ahead to continue or even escalate the teasing, name-calling, or put-downs. Children need to hear us say or indicate "Stop" when their words are hurtful.

Guide students to take responsibility for their words

It's understandable that children (or adults) may try to deflect blame for their words. Students often say, "I was just joking" or "I didn't mean anything by it." You can accept these explanations while still requiring students to take responsibility for the impact of their words. You might say, "I know you were joking, but as we've been discussing in class, sometimes jokes hurt. This is one of those times."

Be clear that hurtful language is not acceptable

When a child publicly teases or puts down a classmate, respond so that all children hear the clear message that such language is not OK. Of course, do so in a way that is direct and respectful to the child. For example, in a calm, even voice you might say, "Brandon, that was unkind" or "Monique, that word is hurtful." This lets all children learn what's acceptable and what's not. If you only respond privately, the child who was hurt and the onlookers may not know you've addressed the issue and might think you found the initial behavior acceptable.

Use logical consequences when appropriate

Sometimes a logical consequence is the appropriate first response to name-calling or teasing because you sense it will be most effective in stopping the behavior and sending a message that the behavior is not acceptable. At other times, you may need to use a consequence because other strategies you tried, such as redirecting a student, failed to stop the unkindness.

Logical Consequences in Action

If a situation like this happens	Try this
During a class discussion, a student shares a family tradition. Another student laughs and says, "That's stupid!"	**Time-out:** "Andre, that was disrespectful. Time-out."
While working at a table with other students, one student says to another, "Is that all you've done? This is so easy. I'm almost finished."	**Loss of privilege:** "Lily, that does not follow our classroom rule of taking care of each other. Work on your own at a private desk for a while. We'll talk later."
A student is thumping his pencil over and over. Finally, a student near him gets angry and says, "Stop it, you idiot! You're driving me bananas!"	**Reparation—"you break it, you fix it":** "John, do over. Ask Anton to stop without calling him a name." Stand close by and wait to make sure John follows through.
During a basketball game at recess, a child says to a teammate who missed a key shot, "You're such a spaz! You just lost the game for us."	**A combination of strategies:** Begin with time-out. "Anna, I know you're upset, but those words were hurtful. Take a break in our cool-down spot. We'll talk later." Later follow up with "you break it, you fix it." "Your words really hurt Zach. You can't take them back, but you can try to make amends. Would you like some ideas for how to do that?"

Encourage apologies; don't force them

When children hurt others' feelings, we teachers often want to order children to apologize. After all, apologizing is the expected response. But we need to resist this urge, because insincere apologies can be as hurtful as the initial unkind words. They won't make an injured child, who can easily see right through them, feel better, and they usually don't help the child who did the teasing become more caring.

Instead of ordering apologies, have the child reflect on the incident. Time-out or loss of privilege can provide that time and space. When you and the child have a private moment, invite him to think about how to apologize or make reparations. However, if the child doesn't want to apologize or make amends, don't force him. Instead, reiterate the expectations for how he should treat others. Then, continue to work with him on empathy, perspective taking, and the power of reparations.

Often, children will apologize or make amends all on their own. These acts are much more meaningful than anything you could force out of a child.

Keep doing proactive work

It's critical to respond to unkind words in the moment. But remember to supplement these in-the-moment responses with the proactive strategies on pages 72–77. After a particular incident, also think about what further support an individual child might need. For example, does she need more opportunities to practice a specific skill, such as knowing the difference between school speech and out-of-school speech? If so, plan ways to build these into her daily schedule. Even a few minutes of extra practice can help.

If a Child Continues to Tease

Despite all your efforts, some students may still engage in teasing, name-calling, or put-downs. If so, here are some things to try.

Check in with the student

Some students may need more than a redirection or consequence to understand the impact of their words and change their behavior. If you think this may be the situation with a particular student, give her some time to reflect and then check in with her privately. Help her understand which class rule she broke, how her words affected classmates, what she thinks she can do to fix the situation, and what she needs to work on for the future.

Form a plan with the student

Sometimes, a student needs more intense and formal support than a check-in meeting. In that case, have a problem-solving conference to invite his ideas about why the problem is happening and to agree on a strategy for changing his behavior. To prepare for the conference, think about:

- ***What to say to begin*** the conference on a positive note.
- ***How to state the problem*** and its impact in concrete terms. For example: "You've been saying unkind things to Eli and Zack. When you make fun of the way they play soccer, it makes them and everyone around them feel unsafe. It also makes people wonder if they can trust you as a friend."
- ***Possible causes of the problem.*** If the child is at a loss as to what's causing his struggles with teasing, name some possible reasons and see if he thinks any ring true. Also, be open to his ideas.
- ***Strategies that may help,*** such as making different choices at recess for a while if that's where the problem is occurring, checking in before and after recess with a teacher, or having a buddy who will try to help. Also, encourage the child to think of some strategies of his own to offer.

Collaborate with colleagues

Ask a colleague to observe the times of day when teasing seems most problematic and then offer insights. Remember also to talk with other teachers who work with the same students you do to ensure you're all consistent in your approach. Discuss how to present a clear message about teasing, promote the use of respectful language, and respond to any unkind words promptly and effectively.

How to Talk With Parents About Teasing

Talking With Parents of Children Who Tease

It's hard on parents when they learn that their child is teasing others. Some parents rush to defend their child or minimize the behavior. Others accept that there's a problem, but they may be at a loss as to how to help their child develop more empathy for others. And some parents might get angry at their child, which can make you worry that the child may be harshly punished if you report any incidents to them.

It can help if, prior to a conversation about teasing, you've told the parents on multiple occasions about the positive attributes you see in their child. Knowing that you're aware of their child's strengths can help parents accept feedback about the teasing. It can also help parents who worry about their child's character keep the issue in perspective.

Parents also tend to react more favorably when teachers describe incidents of unkind words without attributing negative intent to the child or implying that the behavior is a character flaw. Present what occurred matter-of-factly:

> "On several occasions, Ion has called classmates names or said things that insulted them. He called one student a dork and another a dummy. He told another student that she was never going to be any good at basketball. We've been working on using respectful language at school, and I want to keep you in the loop about what we're trying and the consequences when Ion says unkind things."

Finally, be prepared for parents' emotional reactions to what you share and try not to take any feedback personally. It can even help to practice ahead of time what you might say if confronted with some challenging statements from parents, as in the examples below.

Talking With Parents Whose Child Teases Others

If a parent says something like this	Try this
"It's not a big deal. I was teased when I was a kid. It's what kids do. Everything is so politically correct now. You can't say anything without hurting someone's feelings."	**State the facts and stay focused on your reasons for concern:** "While children who were teased may turn out OK, research shows that being teased can cause lasting damage. I want to help everyone in our class avoid that. In terms of T. J., I want to make sure he learns how to interact with classmates successfully."
"Every time we hear about an incident, we punish her. I just don't know why she has to be so mean."	**Acknowledge the parent's positive intentions and focus on nonpunitive strategies:** "It sounds as if you're also trying to help Marcy understand the impact of her words. At this point, I'm thinking that we need some new strategies to use at school. I'm happy to share the approaches we've been trying."
"I think she only teases other people because Aliyah makes her do it. That's the kid you need to focus on."	**Assure the parent that you're taking a comprehensive approach and return the focus to their child:** "I assure you that I'm working with all the students involved. As for Desiree, I'm trying to help her understand that she has the power not to do what other people tell her, and that her words can hurt even if she doesn't mean them to. I think learning both of these things will help her become a stronger person and have better relationships with her classmates."

Talking With Parents of Children Who Are Being Teased

Parents whose child has been teased often feel their child's hurts deeply and want not only to stop the teasing but, in some cases, to make sure the child doing the teasing "gets what he deserves." At the other extreme, some parents worry that their child is too sensitive and won't be able to cope with life's routine setbacks. As you discuss these issues with parents, also be mindful of your obligations to the child who's engaged in the teasing. You'll want to preserve that child's dignity and follow your school's confidentiality policy.

The best place to begin these conversations is with empathy. Often these parents just need us to listen to what their child's experience has been. When they feel heard, they're more open to discussing possible next steps. If, instead, we dispute their child's version of events, minimize what happened, or jump right in with solutions, parents can feel as if we don't truly care about what they have to say.

Sometimes parents report incidents of name-calling or teasing that surprise us. Perhaps we've never seen any signs of discomfort on their child's part. Or the child they name as the person doing the teasing has never shown any such tendencies in front of us. If you need to, bring the conversation to an end at this point to give yourself time to observe, think, and talk to the students involved. You may want to say something like the following:

> "I'm very concerned about what you're saying. This is the first I've heard about this incident, so I'd like to observe recess a few times to see what I can discover and think more about what you've said. If you think Francie would be comfortable, I'd also like to talk with her and hear what she has to say."

Set a time to reconvene with the parents and then go about your observations and research.

As with parents of children who are doing the teasing, the parents of children who are being teased may make statements that seem challenging to you. Try not to become defensive. Instead, listen attentively and be prepared to respond in supportive, yet neutral, ways, as in the examples below.

Talking With Parents Whose Child Is Being Teased

If a parent says something like this	Try this
"It's not a big deal. I was teased when I was a kid. It's what kids do. She just needs to learn to be tougher."	**Acknowledge parents' views, and then refocus on creating a safe learning environment:** "Sometimes teasing isn't something to get overly concerned about, but I've heard some of the things Angie's classmates have said and they're hurtful. I want Angie to develop resilience and also to feel safe and cared for at school."
"The teasing is making him not want to come to school. We've never seen him like this."	**Express empathy and a desire to work together:** "That must be really difficult for Sang and for you. I want to hear more about what's happening so that I can help."
"I don't understand how someone could behave like this and get away with it. Isn't there supervision? Are you too busy to pay attention to what's going on?"	**Assure the parent that you're committed to addressing the problem with them. For example:** "I know how hurtful this has been and I'm sorry it has happened. I wish that I had seen these incidents. Now that I know about them, I want to talk with you about what we're doing to make sure they don't happen again."

Closing Thoughts

Children who tease, children who are teased, and those who are bystanders all need our help. Children who tease are not inherently mean; they just have to find other ways to meet their social-emotional needs. Children who are teased need to know that we will intervene and work to protect them from further meanness. Bystanders to teasing can learn how to support classmates who are being teased and talk in assertive and respectful ways to those who tease.

By understanding teasing, taking proactive steps to prevent it, and responding effectively to any unkind words, we consistently convey our expectations for kindness and respect at school. This can make school life and learning safer and more fulfilling for all students.

Key Points

- Children say mean things in a mistaken attempt to fulfill their needs or because they lack certain social skills.
- Proactively teach children how to use kind language and ensure that everyone can enjoy learning. Teach children to focus on the impact of their words, not their intentions.
- Respond to any teasing, name-calling, or put-downs and encourage students to take responsibility for their words.
- When talking with parents of children who have teased or been teased, acknowledge their concerns and focus on helping their child be safe and successful at school.

3

Cliques

Cliques

From Exclusion to Inclusion

My colleague Sarah Fillion told me a story that may sound familiar to anyone who's dealt with cliques. Day after day, a group of fifth grade girls at the school where Sarah worked battled over who was "in" and who was "out." One day, one of the girls might tell a teacher that the rest of the group wouldn't let her play with them. But the next day, that girl would be back "in." Someone else would then complain that the girl excluded the day before was now being mean to others.

On days when a girl was "out," the group would go to great lengths to create misery for her and get her in trouble. And although the group lacked cohesion, the girls did unite on one issue—certain girls could not ever be part of the group.

While this clique jockeyed for power and control, they made the school day unpleasant for everyone. Whether at recess or lunch, or working on an academic lesson, they created tension and bad feelings among themselves and their classmates. Even students in other grades were affected.

These situations can be hard for us to understand. Why can't these girls just get along? Why not have a happy recess and pleasant lunch? Isn't it exhausting to put that much energy into exclusionary relationships? And to be fair: Excluding others isn't something that only girls do. How boys exclude others may look, sound, and feel different than for girls, but it's still common. For example, a group of boys may try to exclude others from playing at recess because they "aren't that good" or "football is for boys only."

Whatever the reason, being left out hurts. Cliques can cause short- and long-term harm to children's social-emotional well-being and academic performance. They can also have damaging effects on the classroom environment and school community. Fortunately, we teachers, parents, and others who work with children can help reduce exclusionary behaviors and build up a sense of teamwork and community.

In this chapter, we'll explore common causes of children's exclusionary behaviors, proactive steps you can take to encourage inclusiveness, how to respond when children do exclude others, and how to communicate with parents about cliques, including parents of children who are engaging in exclusionary behaviors and those whose children are being excluded.

Why Do Children Form or Join Cliques?

For whatever reason, and at all ages, being part of an exclusive club makes us humans feel special. Starting in childhood, we often identify ourselves as part of certain groups—for example, our families, those who share our ethnic heritage, and those who share our religious beliefs.

As we grow older, many of us continue to seek membership in clubs that exclude others—think of fan clubs, sororities, fraternities, and so on. Businesses also prey on our needs for feeling exclusive by offering us special deals or membership privileges. I was keenly reminded of this on a recent plane trip as I was redirected to the blue carpet because the red carpet was for "premier" passengers only!

Here's a closer look at what's behind most children's exclusionary behaviors.

To feel significant

When children are asked to join an exclusive group, they might think, "I must be special to be invited when others are not." Being part of an exclusive group can also help a child feel less alone or help him form an identity: "They want to play with me." "They think I'm smart." "They understand me." For older students, especially fifth and sixth graders, being in the "popular" group can be particularly important.

To feel powerful

Just by itself, the act of excluding can give children a sense of control. When Lauren tells Sammy, "You can't play with us," she might momentarily feel a thrill from her exercise of power. And if Lauren's behavior goes unchecked, she may realize that she can manipulate other classmates in this way.

To have fun

For some children, the drama that often accompanies cliques can make life seem more exciting. After all, a boring indoor recess or a dull lunch can be magically transformed when some conflict is stirred up! Some children (and adults) have fun at others' expense by creating clubs with complex entrance requirements and exclusive events.

Lack of social skills related to empathy

Some children who exclude others may seem quite skillful in the social arena. After all, they can form a close-knit social group. In reality, however, these children, especially those in kindergarten and first grade, may not yet be able to view things from another person's perspective—including seeing how a person might feel when left out. Some older children and teens may struggle with perspective-taking and empathy as well.

Cliques and child development

Research shows that children begin excluding others and making selective choices about friendships very early in life and that those acts continue well into adulthood. Nonetheless, at certain grade levels, children tend to have some developmental characteristics that make exclusion more likely to occur.

Some Child Development Characteristics Related to Cliques

Grade	Characteristic	Influence on cliques and exclusion
1st (ages 5–7)	• Sometimes tease or are critical of others • Very concerned about having friends; some begin to have "best friends" • Can be very competitive	• Think some children are "lesser" or have qualities they don't like • May see making friends as akin to a competitive sport in which they can win by keeping one friend while excluding another
4th (ages 8–10)	• Often feel worried or anxious • Can be very critical of themselves and others • Like to form small groups • Frequently argue when working in groups	• May feel less anxious and actually comforted by feeling part of an exclusive group • May exclude or form cliques in reaction to disputes, perceived slights, or criticism of others
6th (ages 10–12)	• More concerned with peers and social issues • Very concerned with who's "in" and "out" • Often define themselves and form their identity by who their friends are	• May want to be seen as "in" by excluding or going along with someone else's exclusion • May form cliques as a way of defining who they are (people who dress a certain way, like a certain type of music, etc.)

If you teach one of the grade levels listed in the chart, it's worth taking some extra time to teach being kind to everyone. But remember that promoting an inclusive classroom is the job of all teachers and makes a difference in every grade. In all grades, it's important that we help students understand why excluding others is harmful and teach them positive ways to gain a sense of significance and develop their social skills. The sections that follow will help you do just that.

Moving Beyond Cliques

Proactive Steps to Promote Inclusion

We can do a lot to minimize the formation of cliques in our classrooms. We can begin by setting a clear expectation of inclusion and by giving students opportunities to appreciate one another. By doing so, they'll be less likely to create exclusive clubs, teams, or alliances. Here are some proactive steps to take.

Build a strong classroom community

Get to know students and encourage them to do the same. Cliques and other exclusionary behavior are less likely to occur when students know and care about all—not just some—of their classmates. Give students time to share about their lives and interests, such as during morning meetings and closing circles at the end of the day. Teach them how to listen carefully, ask relevant questions, and show appreciation for what they hear.

Also lead students in games and other activities to foster their connections with each other. For instance, play Four Corners or Maître D' in which students form and re-form different groups to discuss a topic, such as "Who's your favorite character in our read-aloud, and why?" Or, play Human Bingo or Commonalities to enable students to mingle and find out facts about their classmates. (For resources on games and energizers, see page 258.)

Be clear that classroom rules prohibit exclusion

Don't assume children know that exclusion is unacceptable. Instead, be explicit that leaving others out violates class rules about being kind and respecting others. Teach exactly what it looks, sounds, and feels like to include other classmates, especially in recess games, lunchtime conversations, bus seat selection, and other situations that are hotbeds of clique activity.

Effective strategies for this teaching include Interactive Modeling and role-play. These lessons can help students gain a clear understanding of what the rules require of them in real-life situations. To learn more about Interactive Modeling and role-play, see pages 24–25.

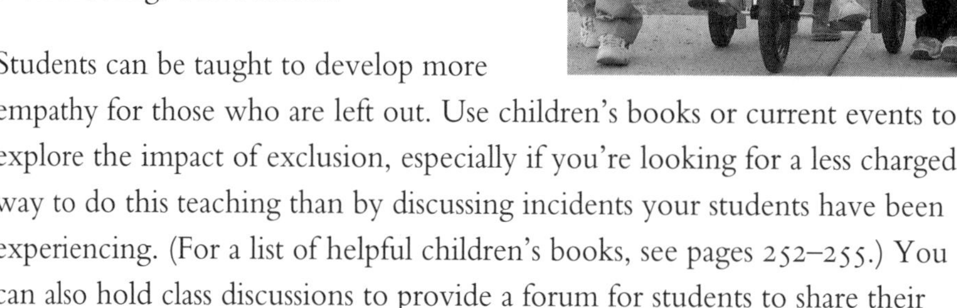

Help students develop empathy for those who are excluded

Students often exclude others to fulfill their own needs but give little or no thought as to how their actions affect others. Some children may even believe that other children's feelings don't matter.

Students can be taught to develop more empathy for those who are left out. Use children's books or current events to explore the impact of exclusion, especially if you're looking for a less charged way to do this teaching than by discussing incidents your students have been experiencing. (For a list of helpful children's books, see pages 252–255.) You can also hold class discussions to provide a forum for students to share their experiences of being excluded (without using the names of students who excluded, of course).

Children will need time and practice to see things from another person's perspective and to develop empathy, so teach them these skills not just once, but continuously.

Assign partners and groups

Use a variety of structures (match up name cards, pick names at random, etc.) to pair students up with different partners in the circle, at learning centers, and at lunch. Rotate partners every week or so. Use a similar process to choose group or team members to ensure that children interact with different classmates.

Avoid putting students in situations where they may feel they have permission to exclude. For example, when left on their own to form a team, children often choose players in ways that make it obvious who's in and who's out.

Observe recess and lunch when you can

Children typically do more excluding during less structured times of the school day, especially lunch and recess. Even if you're not on duty at those times, try to occasionally visit and observe students. Also, check in with colleagues who regularly supervise these times and ask them to alert you to any problems. Work together to promote inclusion and to respond consistantly if exclusion should occur. To further support inclusion, put in place structures such as assigned seats, lunch buddies, and whole-group recess choices.

Reinforce acts of inclusion and kindness

Remember that children are paying attention to what you say and do. By commenting when students reach out to others, you let students know that those acts really do matter. Publicly let the whole class know when you've seen most of them including others. If you notice acts of inclusion by one or two students, point these out privately. (Publicly praising one child can make that child feel uncomfortable, and others who did kind acts but were not seen may feel somewhat excluded themselves.)

Reinforcing Language in Action

For a situation like this	Try this
A child invites a student who usually plays alone at recess to join a game.	**(Privately):** "Ben, I noticed you asked Andru to join you and your friends at recess. You helped him feel like he belonged."
A small group of students who sometimes exclude others join a whole-group game at recess; they successfully interact with multiple classmates during the game.	**(Privately):** "I saw you all join the tag game. I also noticed that everyone followed the rules and played well together. It looked like everyone was feeling included and having fun."

CONTINUED ON PAGE 96

For a situation like this	Try this
During indoor recess, the class plays happily in small groups at a variety of stations. Everyone is included, has something fun to do, and seems content.	**(Publicly):** "That looked like fun. I noticed that you worked hard to make sure everyone had someone to play with. That's following our rule about taking care of each other!"

Reflect with students about their efforts to be inclusive

Occasionally hold a class discussion (after lunch or recess is a good time) about how students are doing, individually and as a class, with inclusiveness. Talk about what they've tried, what's worked, what they're struggling with, and how they're feeling about friendliness in general. These reflections reinforce the message that inclusion is the classroom expectation.

Here are some guidelines for these discussions:

- ***If students need to discuss problems they're having*** with inclusion, remind them not to use names or describe incidents in a way that lets everyone know whom they're discussing.
- ***Hold these discussions to check on general progress*** and continuous issues involving many children. Avoid having a whole-class discussion in response to one particular incident. Instead, address that incident privately with the children involved.
- ***Be sure that all voices are heard*** and, if issues are raised, that children work together toward a solution.
- ***If you suspect bullying*** or unequal power between students around issues of inclusion, don't hold a class discussion to address the incidents. Instead, work individually with the child doing the bullying, following school protocols, and take steps to protect the child who was targeted from further isolation. Meanwhile, teach the whole class general lessons on inclusion so that everyone feels safe and can do their best learning. For bullying prevention and related resources, see pages 256–260.

Show appreciation for all students

Sometimes, without meaning to, we signal to students that we prefer some over others. If we repeatedly make public disparaging comments to the same students, we can diminish their social status. If we joke with some students, but discipline others when they try to joke with us, we show our preferences. Some children may then translate our preferences as permission to exclude those children. Similarly, if we see children continually being excluded and fail to act, we may give the message that those children don't matter.

Donald Graves, who researched, taught, and wrote about the writing process, has described an exercise that you can use as a self-check to see how well you know and express appreciation for your students. Using three columns, note the following:

Column 1	*Column 2*	*Column 3*
Who is in your class? Record not by alphabetical order, but just as students come to your mind.	**What interests each child?** For each student, try to write an interest, hobby, or talent.	**Have I acknowledged this interest?** Put a star if you're sure the child knows you're aware of this special aspect.

Analyze your results. Who came to mind first? Why? Were there any students you could not recall? Were there any for whom you had a hard time filling in column two or three? If so, that's a clear sign that they might need more attention and appreciation.

Teach children how to support those who are excluded

Children may not fully grasp the importance of reaching out to those who are left out. Even if they do, they may not know how. To support children's efforts to reach out:

- ***Teach the distinction between friendliness and being friends.*** Let students know that you expect them to be friendly to everyone, even though they may not become friends with everyone.

➤ ***Teach how to approach others.*** Inviting someone to join a game at recess, sit together at lunch, or be work partners is a complex social skill that children will need a great deal of support to learn. Interactive Modeling and role-play (pages 24–25) are effective ways to teach this skill. Also, see pages 252–255 for a list of children's books that you can use to teach and reinforce this skill.

➤ ***Brainstorm lunch conversation starters.*** Rather than leaving children to their own devices at lunch, when exclusionary behavior often happens, use Interactive Modeling or role-play to teach children how to start a discussion and other conversation skills. For example, model how to find a topic of mutual interest with a partner. You can also follow up on what children learn about each other by playing non-competitive class trivia games at morning meeting or other times.

➤ ***Address what to do if they're rejected.*** Let students know that sometimes when they reach out to someone who's been isolated, that person might say no at first because he's nervous about trusting people. For example, the person might have had classmates be unkind in the past and might be unsure that a new friend really wants to play with him. Or the person might worry that the new friend won't have fun if they play together.

Role-play with children what they can do if their attempts to play, work, or sit with a classmate are rejected. For example, they might want to reapproach the person later and at least keep being friendly toward him. Practice how that might look and sound.

Reach out yourself to students who are socially isolated

Keep an eye out for students who seem to have a hard time fitting in. Notice if a child is sitting alone on the swings, is looking downcast at lunch and not talking to anyone, or is frequently ignored during otherwise social times. These children may be at high risk for being excluded or bullied.

Talk with these students in private to get to know them better and learn what challenges they may be facing. Then, use what you know about all your students to help these children make connections with classmates who you know love the same book series, TV show, or kind of music.

Finally, in addition to whole-class teaching of social skills, such as how to join in a conversation or game, provide one-on-one practice for a child who struggles socially.

When Exclusion Happens

How to Respond Effectively in the Moment

Building a strong community and teaching how exclusion hurts will greatly diminish the chances that children leave others out. But some exclusion is still likely because children often learn by trying out behaviors and seeing what happens. So when children do exclude others, a respectful, matter-of-fact response—through a redirection or a logical consequence—sends a powerful message. It tells both the children doing the excluding and the children being mistreated that in this classroom and school, exclusion is definitely not OK.

Here are some more tips for responding effectively to an incident of exclusion.

Respond promptly

We may not be able to see every incident of exclusion. But we can respond to every incident we do see, even if the incident seems minor. When we do that, we tell the children who were left out that they're not alone in the world, that we care about them, and that we're trying to stop further mistreatment. On the other hand, if we ignore or minimize exclusion, the students who were mistreated will feel even more alone. Worse, we send a message to other students that their exclusionary behavior can continue.

Use logical consequences appropriately

Children who exclude others often need help connecting what they did with its hurtful effects. Some children may also need help learning to value all, not just some, classmates. They may understand that their exclusion was hurtful, but they may not understand how much the other person's feelings matter. Logical consequences can help children build those connections.

Often, you'll want to start with an initial consequence to stop the exclusion in the short term and then follow up with another action to address the situation more fully. For instance, when children engage in exclusion at recess, the initial consequence might be a time-out. An additional consequence may be that they have to play near a recess supervisor for a certain number of days. This lets the teacher make sure that the exclusion has stopped and helps the child fully understand how important inclusion is.

Logical Consequences in Action

If a situation like this happens	Try this
A kindergartner starts to sit down between two classmates in the circle. The classmates refuse to let him sit there because they're saving that seat.	**Time-out:** "David, Anthony, take a break. In this classroom, we include people."
A group of sixth grade girls has formed a clique and are making a list, ranking boys and girls in the class in order of "hotness." You find them working on the list during writing time.	**Start with loss of privilege:** "You've lost the privilege of sitting together. Kaycee, take your things to that table. Amelie, take yours over there. Evie, you stay here. Return to your writing assignment. We'll talk at the end of writing time." **Then follow up:** Consult with an administrator. A clique like this can harm the entire classroom community and writing such a list may need to be reviewed per the school's discipline policy.

If a situation like this happens	Try this
A group of third grade boys tells a girl that she cannot play soccer with them anymore at recess because it's for "boys only" and that girls "suck" at soccer.	**Start with loss of privilege:** "Our rules say we include everyone. You've lost the privilege of playing soccer today and tomorrow." **Follow up later with "you break it, you fix it":** • *Guide understanding:* "What rule did you break? How do you think Kayla felt? What can you do to help repair the situation?" • *Make a plan:* "If you're going to play soccer again, we need to make sure the game is inclusive. Let's talk about that plan."

Encourage apologies; don't force them

Sometimes, especially if you were able to interrupt exclusionary behavior early, children may want to make amends through an immediate apology or other act of reparation. Most students, however, need a little reflection time to get to this point. When you give them this time, they'll be more likely to make amends with a sincere apology or other kind act.

Encourage apologies, but don't pressure students to make them. A forced apology rarely makes the excluded students feel better, as they usually will feel its insincerity. It also doesn't help students who excluded others change their behavior or fully understand the impact of their actions.

What to Do If the Exclusion Continues

Sometimes, children get stuck in exclusionary behaviors, so it will take working with them individually or in small groups to help them move past these behaviors. When students continue to form cliques or exclude others, remember to revisit the proactive strategies on pages 93–99 to reteach and provide additional support. You may also want to try these next steps.

Hold private skills sessions

For children who have formed strong cliques or engaged in repeated exclusionary behaviors, set up a series of private meetings, such as private lunches or before-school chats. At these meetings, discuss and coach children in positive, inclusionary ways to interact with classmates. You might begin these meetings by saying, "I want to make sure you know how to live out our class rule that says we take care of each other. Taking care of each other means including everyone and not making anyone feel left out."

Help students understand the impact of their actions and use Interactive Modeling or role-play to teach them new skills. If you're working with a group of students, guide them in brainstorming and practicing ways to help each other make better choices if old habits resurface. Also challenge students to channel their energy into positive, inclusive social interactions. For instance, you could institute a system with a student in which she reports to you twice a day about acts of kindness she showed or instances when she resisted an urge to exclude.

Conduct a problem-solving conference

You may also want to meet with a student one-on-one to help him develop strategies to meet his needs other than by excluding others. Problem-solving conferences allow you and the child to explore together the kinds of actions he's taking that exclude others, why those behaviors are problematic, and possible causes for and solutions to the misbehavior. In advance of the conference, consider:

- ***How you'll establish rapport*** with the child (for example, think of a positive accomplishment that you can mention).
- ***How to state the problem*** and its impact in concrete terms. For example: "As you know, I've heard from Mr. Ramos that you've been telling people they can't sit with your group at lunch and that they can't play with you at recess. When you exclude people, it makes them feel like they're not part of our school. It also makes

everyone feel less safe because they worry about whether you might be unkind to them next."

- ***Possible causes of the problem.*** If the child is at a loss as to what's causing him to exclude people, name some possible reasons and see if he thinks any ring true. Also, be open to his ideas.
- ***Strategies that may help,*** such as playing with a different group of friends each day, having structured choices at recess, or following a "kindness plan" for lunch. Also encourage the child to think of some strategies of his own to offer.

Collaborate with colleagues

Work with same-grade teachers and other colleagues to agree on a consistent approach to prevent and respond to exclusionary behaviors. For instance, when introducing recess, your grade-level team might put all students together to hear one message about the importance of including everyone and how to do that. Work with colleagues to find age-appropriate children's literature to use to teach inclusion, to design Interactive Modeling lessons or role-plays together, or to structure a whole-class discussion of inclusion.

In some cases, you may even want to hold meetings with colleagues and children from several classes. For instance, if the boys across a grade level are excluding others during sports at recess, one teacher could meet with the boys while another supervises an activity with the girls. It can also be helpful to have a colleague occasionally come watch part of your day when exclusion is a problem. The colleague might be able to offer insights or see subtleties you missed.

How to Talk With Parents About Cliques and Exclusion

Early in the school year, share with parents school and class expectations related to exclusion. You could do this in a letter or at back-to-school night. Give them a broad understanding of why inclusion matters and how it helps every child develop better social-emotional and academic skills. Also, share with parents some of the strategies you use to promote inclusive behavior.

TEACHING TIP

When Parents Encourage Exclusion

A few parents may feel proud that their child is popular and subtly encourage exclusionary behaviors. If you learn of such a situation, avoid responding in a judgmental way. Instead, stay focused on the issue at hand and affirm that a child can be both popular and inclusive.

Throughout the year, if children form cliques or engage in other acts of exclusion, you'll have to communicate this news to parents—parents of children who have been excluding others and, depending on the situation, parents of children who have been excluded. Or the first time you learn of an incident of exclusion might be when a parent contacts you. No matter how you become aware of the situation, be prepared to address it promptly, objectively, and with sensitivity.

Talking to Parents of Children Who Exclude

When parents learn that their child has been excluding others, they may react in different ways. Some parents become defensive. They may feel that their child's friendships are none of our business. They may even speak of their child's "right" to make her own choices and hang out with whomever she wants.

Other families worry about what this behavior reveals about their child's character. They may wonder how their child became so interested in being popular and so uncaring about other children's feelings. Many parents seem to fall somewhere in between—somewhat concerned, but also wondering if you or the school are making too big of a deal of things.

With any parent whose child excludes others, be explicit about what you have noticed (facts only), how the behavior is affecting their child, and how it's hurting others. If parents react angrily, remember that you don't have to convince them to agree with you. Instead, respectfully convey that you appreciate their point of view. Then, explain that it's your job as a member of the school staff to provide a learning environment in which all children feel safe so that they can be successful students.

Talking With Parents Whose Child Excludes Others	
If a parent says something like this	**Try this**
"This sounds like ordinary kid stuff. It's normal for kids to like some kids more than others. I don't expect Kyle to like everyone. That's unrealistic."	**Acknowledge the parent's view; describe the child's specific behavior and the behavior goal:** "You're right. It's common for children to like some classmates more than others. However, when Kyle keeps telling certain boys that they can't play on the only basketball court we have, he's not following our rule of being respectful to everyone. So, I'm suggesting that we work together to help Kyle learn how to maintain his friendships while also playing with all his classmates, even those he may not like."
"We just want you to know that we don't encourage this behavior. When we talk to Tonya about it, it seems as if she doesn't even hear what we're saying."	**Offer reassurance; refocus on solving the problem:** "I doubt it's anything you did or didn't do. Many children experiment with cliques as part of their social development. And sometimes, as we're finding with Tonya, it requires several strategies to help a child move past these behaviors. Why don't I share what I've been trying at school?"
"Other kids do this kind of thing, too. Why are you singling out Wendi?"	**Ask for clarification:** "Could you tell me more about why you think I'm singling out Wendi? That's not my intention." OR **Reassure and then refocus on the child:** "For confidentiality reasons, I can't discuss what's happening with other students. But I want to assure you that I respond right away whenever I see or hear about exclusion. For today, I'd like to discuss how we can help Wendi."

Be prepared in case the conversation becomes personal or highly charged. Keep your cool, so you can respond empathetically and encourage a calm and thoughtful discussion. Remember also that parents are likely to be more accepting of news of exclusion if you've previously told them about their child's positive attributes.

Talking to Parents of Children Who Are Being Excluded

Finding out that their child has been excluded or feels isolated at school can be devastating to some parents. They may question whether they have given their child what he needs to succeed socially or whether they could have done something to prevent the pain their child has experienced. So be sensitive. You need to convey the facts so that parents fully understand the situation, but perhaps you don't need to relay every detail about every incident.

If parents tell you about an incident that you were unaware of, let them finish what they have to say before responding. Refrain from jumping in too quickly or becoming defensive. Be especially careful not to imply that it's the child's fault he's being excluded.

Also, if you're learning about an incident of exclusion for the first time from parents, you may want to suggest that you take some time to talk to their child and observe the times of day when the exclusion is occurring. Although our teacher instinct is often to solve problems immediately, we're more likely to succeed if we first observe and consider the full measure of the situation. Again, be prepared for some conversations to feel personal. Try to maintain an empathetic and thoughtful response to what parents say.

Talking With Parents Whose Child Is Being Excluded	
If a parent says something like this	**Try this**
"This is my fault. I work so much that we don't have time to invite other children over. I also don't let him watch TV, so he doesn't know about some of the same things his classmates do."	**Emphasize it's never the excluded child's fault; refocus on solving the problem:** "I assure you that it's not your fault or Ken's. Excluding other people is never OK; that's what we teach. I'm working with the students who were mean to Ken and helping the whole class get to know him better."
"She's feeling bad about her clothes. She thinks that if she looked different, they'd let her sit with them at lunch. We just don't have the money to buy the kinds of clothes and things those girls have."	**Express empathy; reassure that you're addressing the problem:** "I'm so sorry this happened. I know how hard it is and want to reassure you that I'm working to stop the mean behavior. Let's make a plan to stay in touch."
"This has been happening since kindergarten. That girl Kerry has tried to be the queen bee since day one, and the school has done nothing about it."	**Acknowledge feelings; reassure that you're addressing the problem; refocus on child:** "I know this has been frustrating. It's the first I've heard of a clique forming. I can't discuss how I'm addressing Kerry's behavior, but I can assure you it's being addressed. Getting back to Lara, what do you think would help her going forward?"

If parents ask for advice on how to promote more inclusionary behaviors in their children, here are some ideas to share:

Ideas to Share With Parents	
Parents of Younger Students	**Parents of Older Students**
• For play dates, occasionally invite a classmate whom the child doesn't usually play or work with at school.	• Consider monitoring the child's use of social media for signs of excluding others or being excluded, such as "unfriending" or saying derogatory things on Facebook.
• For birthday parties, try to be as inclusive as possible. If unable to invite everyone, talk with the child and guests about how to be considerate of the feelings of those not invited.	• Encourage the child to try different activities and hobbies. These provide opportunities to develop new skills and interact with a variety of children.

For All Parents

- If a child uses derogatory language about classmates to justify exclusion, listen closely to understand his or her point of view. But also encourage a kinder and more open-minded viewpoint.
- If a child complains of being left out or talks about excluding others, let me know. That way, we can work together as a team to address any concerns.

Closing Thoughts

One night while driving home from work, I heard a recorded interview of one of my favorite singers, the late Janis Joplin. In the interview, she talked about how painful her high school years were. She never felt that she fit in; often she was teased and excluded at school.

Even though Joplin was wildly popular and these incidents had occurred years before the interview, I was struck by the obvious pain in her voice.

It was a helpful reminder to me that addressing cliques and exclusion can feel like a long climb up a steep mountain, but it's a climb we must undertake for the sake of our children. It will make such a difference in their lives and the lives of those they come into contact with.

Every time we step in when children have been isolated or excluded, we tell them that they do matter and that someone does care about them. And we help students who are doing the excluding learn more about tolerance, kindness, and the expectations of a civil society.

Key Points

 Children may form cliques and exclude classmates in other ways because it makes them feel special and powerful.

 Tell children that exclusion is never OK. Take proactive steps to promote inclusion, such as teaching children how to invite others to join them at recess and lunch.

 Respond to any incidents of exclusion right away; encourage students to apologize or make other amends, but don't force them to do so.

 Keep parents informed of the proactive steps you're taking to promote inclusion and about any incidents of exclusion. Be empathetic and keep the focus on helping their children succeed in school.

4

Tattling

Tattling

Rethinking "No Tattling" Rules

During a busy day of teaching, constant reports by students about what other students are doing wrong can really fray a teacher's nerves.

"Freddie is not on the right page!" "Sara hit me!" "Josh said the s-word." "Emily got water on the floor and didn't clean it up."

Dealing with these sorts of complaints—what we commonly call "tattling"—can take a significant amount of time and energy every day. As a result, tattling has often been treated like any other rule-breaking behavior. Teachers often actively discourage tattling or even ban it, telling children to "mind their own business." When children disregard these bans and report incidents to teachers anyway, we often respond negatively ("Don't be a tattletale. Get back to your seat.") or even impose a consequence.

However, it's a mistake to lump the reporting of problematic incidents in with other misbehaviors or, worse yet, to view children who report them in a negative light.

Often, children who are reporting incidents to us are trying to figure out what the rules mean and how to develop their own self-control. Sometimes they're trying to show us that they really know the rules. And while they may sometimes report incidents that seem insignificant to us ("Leo is in the wrong spot in line"), often they're telling us about themselves or another child being truly hurt ("Leo keeps pushing me whenever we line up").

This information is helpful for us to know to keep our classrooms safe. Reporting such incidents is not a behavior we should discourage or one for which reprimands or consequences are warranted. Moreover, if we treat "tattling" as a misbehavior and discourage children from reporting, they may refrain from telling us about any problem behaviors. And when relatively small incidents of physical or emotional aggression go unchecked, they often escalate into bigger problems such as bullying.

Our goal, then, should not be to eliminate children's reporting of incidents, but to replace a "no tattling" rule with a more nuanced, but more practical, set of guidelines about reporting—and then teach these guidelines to students.

In this chapter, you'll learn how to do that, along with how to respond when children do report minor incidents so that you don't inadvertently discourage them from telling you of the serious ones. You'll also learn how to reframe and address "tattling" with parents so that they better understand your approach to reporting.

Why Do Children Report?

The reasons children tell adults about incidents are varied and complex. When they or someone else is hurt, physically or emotionally, telling an adult is a logical step for getting help. At other times, children tell us what other people did because they're still figuring out the rules and learning how they apply. Students may also report minor incidents because they lack the skills to handle them any other way.

To get help

If children see one child hitting another, taking someone's lunch, ordering people not to play with someone, or doing something else unsafe or unkind, they need to tell someone who can help. This is comparable to adults reporting troubling incidents to the police, a supervisor at work, or a trusted colleague. We may wish children didn't report so many incidents to us (perhaps because we're feeling overwhelmed), but the reality is that in many situations reporting is the right thing for children to do.

A form of self-regulation

Sometimes, children tell us when other children break the rules even if those behaviors do not involve emotional or physical hurt. This type of reporting is often a child's way of figuring out what the rules actually mean. Developmental psychologists call this process "other regulation"—that is, one way children learn to regulate themselves is by regulating others.

This reporting of others' rule-breaking behavior reminds me of when I was learning to play basketball as a young girl. I'd watch games and complain out loud if the referee didn't call certain fouls. Verbalizing the players' rule violations helped me to fully understand the rules of the game. Likewise, reporting what other students did wrong helps children learn and master the rules of the classroom.

To feel significant

In other situations, children report to us because it helps fuel their need for significance. Maybe they want us to recognize them more and show us that they, unlike some students, know and appreciate the rules. Maybe they want their classmates to see them as knowledgeable in this area. Even now, as an adult, I must confess that I sometimes yell at the referee to show my sports-loving husband that I also know quite a few things about the game of basketball!

A lack of skills

For some students, overreporting is related to a lack of certain social skills. They may encounter situations that they could easily resolve or ignore, but they don't yet know how to do so. For example, when I taught kindergarten, some children would tell me that another student wanted the same marker they did. My first (silent) thought was "Seriously?" But, my calmer self thought, "Wow, I need to spend more time teaching them how to share!" Sometimes, children have no strategy to fall back on other than telling an adult.

Reporting and child development

As children rise through the elementary grades, they report incidents less and less frequently, whether for developmental reasons or because they've learned not to report. Developmentally, children in younger grades are often more interested in the approval of their teachers, which can lead them to tell us about many (or all) of the rule-breaking behaviors they see. Young children are also more literal; they may have a harder time discerning what to report, and what to handle on their own or ignore.

Some Child Development Characteristics Related to Overreporting		
Grade	**Characteristic**	**Influence on overreporting**
Kindergarten (ages 4–6)	• Often seek adult approval • Can be very literal and see only one way to do things	• Want adults to recognize they know the rules • Get upset when others don't do things the way they think they should
1st (ages 5–7)	• Anxious to do well • Sometimes tease or are critical of others • Often complain	• Want adults to recognize they know the rules • Striving to figure out the rules by criticizing and complaining about others
2nd (ages 6–8)	• Can be moody or sensitive • Thrive on security and structure • Often quite conscientious and serious	• More likely to find fault with those around them • Get upset when others don't follow the rules • Take the rules seriously and try to help by telling the teacher of infractions

Although overreporting is more likely to occur in younger grades, it still does occur in the older grades, so it's important to teach all children what to report and how. For older children, also be aware that underreporting may be an issue. These children will need you to teach just how important reporting is in certain situations.

When we take the time to guide students on when and how to report, we help them move toward greater autonomy and responsibility. We'll also have fewer distractions in our classrooms, allowing us more time for teaching and students more time for learning.

Should I Tell or Not?

Proactive Steps for Teaching How to Report

If children feel that they can't report teasing, excluding, physical aggression, or other potentially dangerous behaviors, they may worry about their safety and lose focus on their learning. However, if children tell you everything, you'll rarely be able to teach without being interrupted. With some thoughtful planning, you can help children learn what, when, and how to report, and how to handle things on their own or to ignore them.

Start with some self-reflection

For many of us raised in a "no tattling" culture, shifting to a more nuanced view may be challenging. It helps to think through what your new approach, including your language, will be. Given that the word "tattling" has negative connotations, think about neutral terms to use in the classroom instead, such as "reporting" or "letting an adult know." You may also want to think through the types of incidents students typically report to you. Which ones do you need to know about? Which ones should they ultimately handle on their own, or ignore? It's also worthwhile, of course, to discuss issues related to reporting with your colleagues.

Build a caring classroom community

When children feel that others care about them, they can more easily tell whether or not classmates' behaviors are problematic. They're also more forgiving of others' mistakes and require less attention from you. Take time to cultivate a community where children know and care about each other. Have students share important information about their lives, play games in which they reveal likes and dislikes, and give children plenty of chances to greet, share, and talk with everyone, not just close friends.

Communicate clear expectations

Once you have a firm understanding of your expectations for reporting, share those with students.

➤ ***Connect class rules to reporting.*** Ideally, as discussed on pages 21–23, one rule should encourage students to take care of themselves; another rule should encourage them to take care of each other. Use these rules as a starting point to discuss with children what they should do if they're being hurt or see someone else being hurt, either physically or emotionally. Tell children that one strategy they can use in situations like these is to tell an adult. If that adult doesn't help, they should tell another adult.

➤ ***Address misconceptions about reporting.*** Many children think that "tattling" is bad and some may even have been encouraged not to tell teachers about serious incidents. Be clear that your views may be different from those of other adults. For example:

> "Some teachers and other adults may have told you not to tattle. But I want you to know that there will be many times when I'll want you to tell me about behaviors that you notice. Today, we'll begin talking about how you'll know when to tell me."

➤ ***Discourage use of "tattling" or "tattletale."*** Discuss with students how people often use these words in unkind ways. Let students know that you'll be teaching them new vocabulary that will help them follow the class rules. For example:

> "Sometimes when children tell adults about something they've seen, other people might call it 'tattling,' call them a 'tattletale,' and make them feel bad. But in our class, our rule says we'll take care of each other, and sometimes that means you'll need to tell an adult about behaviors that you see. Today we'll talk about a word to use instead of 'tattling'—'reporting.'"

Help students know what to report

Children will need a great deal of teaching to understand why they should report certain incidents, but not others. A simple way to do this is to brainstorm common events with students. Then, for each incident, guide students in discussing what action to take and why. You might want to use a chart like the one on the following page to list their ideas.

Let an adult know	Handle it yourself	Let it go
(when someone's body or feelings are hurt; when in doubt, report)	(when there's a conflict, but no one's body or feelings are hurt)	(when someone made a mistake, but it didn't cause a conflict or hurt anyone's body or feelings)
• someone threatens to hit you • someone calls your friend an unkind name • someone tells you that you can't play because you're not part of their group • someone keeps bumping into you and knocking you down during tag • some older kids are blocking the door of the bathroom and not letting younger students in	• you want the same marker as someone else • you and a friend disagree about what to do at play time • someone bumps into you while playing tag • someone sits in your spot on the rug	• someone uses a marker instead of a pencil • someone is not doing her work • someone is not doing his classroom job • someone reads a comic book instead of writing during writing workshop

As you discuss the incidents, be aware of your students' tendencies. If you teach younger students, guide them not to put everything in the "let an adult know" category. But older students, who often err on the side of underreporting, might need encouragement to put some instances in that category. Also acknowledge that context matters—a bump in a soccer game may feel like it's no big deal, but in other situations, it may feel like an act of aggression. Over time, children need to learn such nuances, both for reporting reasons and also for their own social development.

Teach students to talk with each other if they're unsure what to do when an incident occurs. Then, if they're still in doubt, they should definitely tell you. In addition, be sure the teaching you do about reporting is consistent with your school's discipline policies.

Give students communication options

Offering students choices for how to share their concerns can increase the likelihood that they'll report serious incidents. It can also help reduce interruptions to your teaching. Here are some ideas to consider:

- ***Secret signal.*** Teach students a simple signal to let you know that they have a concern to report. For older children, an inconspicuous signal can also allow them to inform you of problems confidentially. Of course, if a student gives you the signal, follow up with her as soon as you can.
- ***Conversation journals.*** Keep "conversation journals" with students in which they write to you daily or a few times a week, and you respond. Students can use these journals for multiple purposes, including telling you of important incidents.
- **Concerns box.** Teach children to write any concerns on slips of paper and drop those into a designated box. Allow them to choose whether to write these concerns anonymously or use their names.
- ***Making appointments.*** Have students make appointments to talk with you in private, using a sign-up sheet or an appointment book. Let students know they can use these appointments to discuss any concern, not just serious incidents.

Of course, remind students that for emergencies (bleeding, vomiting, etc.), they should always tell you right away.

Teach students how to let things go

If we want children to ignore truly minor issues, we have to teach them what this looks, sounds, and feels like. Use strategies such as Interactive Modeling and role-play to do this teaching. For example, teach children how to use self-talk or a movement such as sitting on their hands to con-

TEACHING TIP

Be Positive

In many ways, we reap what we sow as teachers. If we focus on what students did wrong, they'll believe that's what we value and start to point out other children's misdeeds to us. If, instead, we spend more time noticing and commenting upon what students do well, students will do the same.

trol their impulse to tell you about an incident that, while annoying, is not hurting them or others. (For more on Interactive Modeling and role-play, see pages 24–25; see pages 234–238 for teaching similar skills related to handling disappointment.)

Teach students problem-solving skills

While there are many issues that children will need our help to resolve, they can usually learn how to handle smaller issues on their own. Here are some simple problem-solving skills to teach:

- ***Telling someone to stop.*** Use Interactive Modeling or role-play to teach students how to tell a classmate respectfully to stop doing something that's bothering them or someone else.
- ***Helping someone who's being treated unkindly.*** Use Interactive Modeling or role-play to teach children how to help someone who's being mistreated, such as by standing next to her or asking if she's OK. Of course, remind children that they should also report incidents of mean behavior to you or another adult.
- ***Sharing materials.*** Many children need to be taught what to do if two or more children want the same book or supply at the same time. Teach them different ways to share materials, such as taking turns or finding an acceptable alternative material.
- ***Conflict resolution.*** Children can learn how to resolve certain disagreements through conflict resolution. Scaffold your teaching of this process, going over each step and supporting students as they practice it. Over time, children can internalize this process and thus be equipped to handle more issues on their own.

One note of caution: In situations of bullying (that is, when there's a power imbalance between students), conflict resolution is not appropriate and can lead to further problems. In these situations, be ready to intervene.

Reinforce students' efforts at following reporting guidelines

Be sure to acknowledge children when they let you know that someone's emotional or physical safety was at risk, when you see them solving problems appropriately on their own, and when they ignore minor behaviors. Name specifically what they did that was helpful and, when an incident requires further action, reassure the child that you'll take care of it.

Reinforcing Language in Action

For a situation like this	Try this (in private)
José tells you that another student is taking someone's lunch every day.	"Telling me this took courage. You did the right thing, José. Now it's my job to solve this problem."
Felicity lets you know that at recess three classmates formed a club and told her that she could not join it.	"That must have hurt your feelings, Felicity. Now that you have told me this, I can help. I'm going to talk with the recess supervisor and also with each girl. Then, we'll talk again."
Andre is trying to tell Dani that she's breaking the rules by not keeping the computer mouse on the pad. Dani ignores him. Andre hesitates but then lets the minor issue go.	"Andre, I saw how you tried to help Dani remember the mouse pad rule. But when she ignored you, you just let it go. That's exactly what we talked about doing when someone isn't hurting anyone. What helped you let this incident go?"
Fareed ordinarily seeks help solving any problem that arises. Today, when Luis takes a book from his desk, Fareed respectfully says, "I wasn't finished with that yet." Luis puts the book back and finds another one.	"Fareed, I saw you handle who got to use the book exactly the way we practiced. You were respectful but told Luis that you weren't finished with it. How did it feel to handle that without my help?"

Review and reteach

Children will need multiple lessons to internalize the concepts of when to report and when not to. During a class discussion (after recess or lunch are good times for these), have students reflect on:

- whether they've reported behaviors adults need to know about
- how easy or hard it's been to know when to handle something themselves
- what they've learned about letting things go

Based on these discussions, add to or revise the class chart of what to report, handle, and let go. Conclude your conversations by emphasizing that, when in doubt, children should tell an adult about any incident that concerns them.

When Children Overreport

How to Respond Effectively in the Moment

Given that our goal is for children to err on the side of telling us about events, we need to respond carefully when they report events that are truly minor. After all, we don't want to inadvertently discourage their reporting altogether. Here are some tips for responding effectively when children overreport.

Assume positive motivation

It's much easier to respond calmly and respectfully to a child's overreporting when you assume good intentions. If, instead, you assume that a child is trying to avoid work or get someone else in trouble, you may respond in ways that discourage future reporting. Keep in mind that children often report small incidents to show us that they know the rules or are knowledgeable about some topic.

Offer affirmation

Preparing some responses in advance can help you give the child who's overreporting some needed affirmation and avoid saying anything discouraging. For example:

- "I see you know the rule about __________."
- "You really know our rules."
- "Oh, you're right. I did say that's how we should __________ (line up, sharpen pencils, etc.). I'll watch that more closely next time."

Avoid sounding judgmental

Although it can be challenging, maintain a calm demeanor when responding. This will help you steer clear of using words or a tone that might make the child feel as if she's done something wrong. Some phrases to avoid: "Why are you telling me this?" "That's not the kind of thing you should be telling me!" and "How is that a problem?"

Don't use consequences

Even when a child reports minor incidents to you, don't give a consequence such as time-out or loss of privilege. Consequences are not appropriate because the message we send to students should be for them to always err on the side of reporting.

If a Child Continues to Overreport

With your proactive teaching, most children will be able to strike a healthy balance between telling you of important incidents and letting go of, or solving, less important ones. Most likely, however, you'll still have a few students who have a hard time managing these distinctions. Revisit some of the proactive strategies on pages 116–122. In addition, some strategies to try to provide extra support follow on the next page.

Find ways to give more affirmation

Some students overreport because they're not feeling significant or noticed. Try to find other ways to address this need. For example, offer them special responsibilities in the classroom, give them opportunities to be a leader, point out the positives you see, or write them an occasional note letting them know you've noticed their efforts.

Teach a nonverbal signal

Some students may benefit from using a nonverbal signal to show you when they've handled an issue on their own or let something go. Then, a simple nod or smile from you will show them that you recognize their self-control and improving social skills.

Provide extra practice

As is true with academic skills, some children may need individual support and practice to distinguish between reportable incidents and those that can be handled independently or ignored. Meet one-on-one or, if you have a few students who need extra support, in a small group to provide more opportunities for sorting out situations and deciding what to do in a given scenario.

Hold a problem-solving conference

Sometimes children need a more structured conversation to address overreporting. In a problem-solving conference with the student, you can delve more deeply into why she might be feeling the need to tell you what her classmates are doing wrong. Also, explore with her concrete strategies she might use to make different decisions.

Because we don't want to discourage children from reporting significant problems, plan for this conference carefully. Think about:

- ***How you will reinforce something the student is doing well.*** This will help set a positive tone for the conversation.
- ***How to state the problem without discouraging reporting.*** For example: "When you or a classmate gets hurt, you tell me and that's really helpful. But sometimes you tell me about things when no one gets hurt. For instance, last week you told me that Kylie didn't eat all her lunch and that Destiny said she hated homework."
- ***Possible causes of the problem.*** If the child is at a loss as to what's causing her to overreport, name a few possible reasons and see if any ring true. Remain open to reasons the child suggests as well.
- ***Strategies to help the child make better choices about what to report.*** For example, you might try a reporting notebook in which she writes down any incidents. Then, the two of you sort what's written. Or, you might suggest she team up with a buddy who could help her decide what to report, according to criteria you've taught. Also ask the child for ideas about what would help her.

Work with colleagues

If a child continues to overreport, ask colleagues who also teach her whether it happens in their classes as well. If it doesn't, try to figure out what might account for the difference. If it does, work together to make sure you each respond consistently. It may also help to ask a colleague to observe a time of day when the student is particularly likely to overreport and then offer insights.

If Students Underreport

Some teachers, often those of older students, face a different challenge—their students rarely tell them about incidents that involve emotional or physical harm. If you think students are not telling you of serious incidents, consider these steps:

- ***Spend some time observing*** the social dynamics of the classroom. Is there a general sense of trust among all students, or are there cliques or certain students who dominate? Sometimes children underreport because they fear reprisal from classmates. You may need to devote more time to fostering a trusting classroom community.
- ***Share your concerns directly with students.*** You might say, "In the last month, I've learned about several serious incidents where people were hurt, well after they occurred. I want to make sure everyone knows how important it is to let me or another adult know of incidents like these right away so we can help."
- ***Invite students' input and ideas.*** Invite students to share what might be getting in the way of their reporting and strategize how to solve the problem.
- ***Reteach what to report.*** Return to the ideas on pages 117–118 to make sure students know the difference between incidents they should report and those they should ignore or handle on their own.
- ***Check in frequently.*** Return to this issue regularly to see how students are feeling about reporting and have them evaluate how they are doing with it.

How to Talk With Parents About Reporting

Parents may also need our help in developing a more nuanced view of tattling versus reporting, and how they can support their child in learning the difference. A few simple steps can help.

Keep parents informed

Talk about your approach to reporting at back-to-school nights; through newsletters, phone calls, and conferences; and on your school or class website. Explain why you want children to err on the side of reporting and what types of incidents are particularly important to report. Share what you're teaching children to do so that parents can support that teaching at home.

Sample Letter to Parents

Dear Parents,

This week, the children and I discussed what to do if they see others breaking rules. We talked about how the rule "Take care of each other" means trying to help classmates who are being treated unkindly. We also talked about the kinds of incidents they need to tell me or another adult about—and the ones they can handle on their own or ignore. For example:

TELL AN ADULT	HANDLE IT YOURSELF	LET IT GO
• Someone bumps into you every time you get in line. • Someone calls you names.	• You and another student want the same marker. • Someone bumps into you by mistake.	• Someone is holding a book upside down. • Someone is reading when she's supposed to be doing math.

Although many adults have learned that "tattling" is bad, I'm trying to teach a different message: that children should tell me whenever they or classmates have been hurt emotionally or physically. This helps everyone stay safe and focused on learning. It helps prevent bullying, teasing, and exclusion. In addition, I'm teaching children not to use the word "tattle" and to use "report" instead. This way, children can learn to err on the side of taking care of themselves and others. Please let me know if you have any questions.

Just as with children, addressing the issue once with parents will probably not be enough. You may need to revisit this topic with all or some parents throughout the school year.

Work with parents whose children overreport

If a child continues to tell you of insignificant incidents, you may want to confer with her parents. Begin by informing them of what you've noticed and the ways you're trying to support the child. For example:

> "As you know, I encourage children to tell me when they or someone else is hurt, but often the incidents Jenna reports don't fall in this category. Today she told me that Maria used too many paper towels in the bathroom and that Angie didn't hang her backpack on the hook. I've been discussing different scenarios and doing some problem-solving with Jenna, but I'd like to hear your ideas about how we can help Jenna in this area."

As always, if you have already been in regular communication with parents about their child's positive attributes, they'll likely be more receptive to a discussion about overreporting.

If students underreport

Despite careful teaching, children may still not tell us about important incidents, although they may tell their parents. Communicate to parents the same message you're giving students—if someone is being physically or emotionally hurt, parents should tell you about it. Give this message more than once to make sure parents know you mean it—for instance, at back-to-school night, in letters home, and at parent-teacher conferences.

You might say to parents, "I want to hear about any issues that come up for your child at school. If he's worried about something or he's facing difficulties, those worries will affect his learning. So, even if you think the worries are minor, please share them with me."

For more information on bullying prevention and related resources, see pages 256–260.

Closing Thoughts

The concept of "no tattling" has negatively affected our efforts to know what's going on in school and keep our students safe. While we may not want students to tell us every little thing, we do want to create a culture in which they tell us about the important issues. With proactive work and a positive classroom environment, we can instill in students an understanding of the difference between what adults need to know and what children can and should be able to resolve on their own.

Key Points

- Children may overreport to show what they know or because they lack the ability to distinguish minor incidents from major ones.
- Take proactive steps to teach children what kinds of incidents they should always report to adults and what they can ignore or handle on their own.
- Respond to overreporting respectfully and assume that children have positive intentions for doing so.
- Tell children to always report an incident to you if they're unsure about what to do.
- Frequently remind parents of the reporting guidelines you're teaching students. Keep the lines of communication open with them on this topic.

5

Defiance

Defiance

Reaching Children Who Struggle With Authority

Children who defy us often get to the core of our fears as teachers. They make us question our abilities and provoke feelings of insignificance. But when we rise above our own feelings and find ways to appreciate these children, we offer them a path to success and a model of how to get along in the world.

I once taught a second grader who sometimes subtly refused to go along with what we were doing. For instance, if it was time to leave the classroom and John didn't want to go, he would get in line—but then walk as slowly as possible. The more his classmates and I urged him to walk faster, the slower he would go. At each of his deliberate steps, I could feel my blood pressure rise. In that moment, there was little I could do. I couldn't physically make

John walk faster and in that moment he couldn't rationally discuss his feelings or options. It was rare for a student's behavior to get to me, but John's resistance always did.

Amelia, a sixth grader, was more classic in her defiance. When presented with an assignment that she found less than engaging, she'd say, "I'm not going to do that. It's a waste of my time." One day, when a colleague asked her to go to the back of the line as a consequence for a rule-breaking behavior, Amelia sat down and refused to move. It was, she said, "a personal sit-in."

When students refuse to follow our lead, it's easy for strong emotions to overtake us. A child who defies authority is often trying to feel significant, but ironically her defiance threatens our own need to feel important. As we both strive to feel significant, it's easy to get enmeshed in a power struggle.

How do you know you're in a power struggle? You feel like you're being tested (which you are) and you get angry. You may even want to dominate the child to prove that you're the boss. But teachers never win power struggles. Once you're in one, you've lost. No one wins a power struggle.

What works best with a child who defies authority is calmly working with him in ways that honor his genuine need to feel significant. It's also critical to demonstrate that you still hold him (and everyone in the class) accountable for following the rules. In this chapter, you'll learn how to do that while keeping your cool.

We'll explore why children defy adults, proactive steps to take to foster cooperation, how to respond to avoid power struggles and restore the student to cooperation, and how to communicate with parents about defiance and help them better understand this issue.

Why Do Children Defy Authority?

We may think that students use defiant behavior to get our goat or ruin our day. But their acts of defiance rarely have much to do with us. The more you can focus on the real reasons students engage in defiance, the more you'll be able to maintain your cool. As you stay in control, you'll likely handle the situation more effectively and help these children learn.

Unmet physical needs

One simple reason children show defiant behavior is that they're hungry or tired. Because they have less energy, it's harder for them to regulate their behavior. They may feel it's easier to refuse than to cooperate, so they'll ignore us or refuse to follow directions.

Academic challenges

Some students refuse to do assignments or follow directions to hide their fear or inability to do what's being asked, such as solving a math problem or reading a passage from a book. They would rather be seen as defiant than incapable, especially in front of their peers.

A sense of significance

Every child needs to feel significant, but sometimes they feel as if they don't fit in at school or that they aren't as important as they'd like to be. Children who struggle academically or socially may believe that they're "bad" students and thus not valued. Regardless of the causes of these beliefs, children may use defiance as a way to gain a sense of personal importance. In contrast, children who feel significant are usually more cooperative.

A need for more control

Sometimes what we say and do unintentionally diminishes a child's feelings of significance. We may be too controlling, rarely offering students responsibilities or choices, and some students may rebel in an attempt to assert the power being denied them. Even more problematically, we may find

ourselves being even more controlling with children who defy us, leading them to rebel more—and starting a frustrating cycle of our trying to impose more control and receiving back from them more defiance.

A need for more attention

Some children have come to learn that defiance can bring them extra attention from teachers and classmates alike—even if that attention is negative. Some classmates may openly admire (and imitate) the courage of these students; others may chastise them. Either way, their teacher and classmates are paying attention to them! Repeating the behavior can become a game: "Watch this," you can imagine a student thinking. Also, if children feel that we give special privileges to others, but not to them, they may use defiance to gain recognition.

Testing limits

Testing limits is a natural part of childhood, and some children need to test them more than others. Children may defy us because they're trying to figure out what will happen. Do we mean what we say, or not? What are we going to do if they don't cooperate? Author Robert Mackenzie coined a descriptive term for these children: "aggressive researchers." These children thoroughly test adults to find out where the limits are and whether we can be trusted to keep our word. Our job then is to give them the information they seek—by consistently sticking to the limits.

Defiance and child development

At certain ages, children are more likely to defy us and take active, even aggressive, steps to test the limits we've set. At other ages, children are more tuned in to issues of fairness and are likely to push back when they sense an adult is being unjust. The table on the next page shows some times when children may be more likely to test limits and defy adults.

Some Child Development Characteristics Related to Defiance		
Grade	Characteristic	Influence on defiance
Kindergarten (ages 4–6)	• Unsure whether to be bad or good • Complain; oppositional • Test limits	• Want to see what happens when they don't cooperate • Feel very unsure of themselves and find defiance a way to assert significance
1st (ages 5–7)	• Struggle accepting responsibility for misbehavior • Easily upset when hurt • Complain frequently	• Have difficulty accepting any negative feedback and so lash out • Complain when the teacher gives a directive that appears controlling
4th (ages 8–10)	• Moody, impatient, negative • Critical of self and others; sensitive to criticism • Very concerned about fairness and justice	• May assume negative intentions on the part of the teacher and feel personally offended • May question own importance and feel threatened when asked to go along with the group • May feel as if the teacher is singling them out unfairly
6th (ages 10–12)	• Like to challenge rules and test limits • Enjoy arguing and debating • Worry about who's "in" and who's "out"	• May want to see what happens if they don't do what the teacher says • May want to impress peers or be encouraged by peers to rebel • May enjoy the act of arguing with the teacher

If you teach one of the grades listed, expect some limit-testing as a natural part of child development. Remember, however, that each child develops in unique ways. One child might not ever go through an oppositional phase; another child may go through these phases in different grades. Regardless of what grade you teach, be ready to help children move from defiance to cooperation. This chapter gives you some practical ideas for how to do that.

Less Defiance, More Cooperation

Proactive Steps to Take

With children who struggle to cooperate, the more you can do proactively to fully engage them, the more successful they will be in staying out of defiance mode. When a student realizes that he can have personal power in positive ways, he'll naturally be more cooperative. He'll also have stronger relationships with peers because they'll feel safer around him. Here are some proactive steps to take.

Check physical needs

It may be helpful to investigate whether lack of food or sleep is leading to instances of defiance. If you notice a child is more resistant at certain times, it may mean that he's hungry. Talk with the child about this possibility or provide him with a snack. Similarly, check with a child's parents to see if there are any sleep issues, particularly if he veers between cooperation and defiance, depending upon the day. If so, try to build in extra rest times during the school day.

Build positive, one-on-one relationships

While this advice applies to all students, it's crucial for students who tend to act defiantly. These children need to feel your unconditional love—that despite any difficulties you'll still care about them, recognize their successes, and actively include them in the classroom community. Look for opportunities to ask students about their lives and show that you care about them.

Remind yourself that every child has positive attributes, including those who frustrate you. As you begin to discover a child's interests and talents, help her channel these in ways that foster her sense of significance. One teacher discovered that a student who frequently resisted her had a gift for mechanics. So during choice time, the teacher began offering her the option of working on small appliances. Her classmates quickly recognized her skills and asked for her help. This small change didn't mean that the two of them never had any more disagreements, but it did help this child feel recognized for her successes.

Reinforce progress and effort

All children need to hear when they're doing well and where they're improving, but this is especially true of children who struggle with defiance. Make it a point to notice the child's successes (big and small), in following directions, making a smooth transition, or doing anything that ordinarily might invite resistance. Reinforce in private—to avoid calling unwanted attention to the child and comparisons with other classmates—and be specific. Whenever possible, follow up with how that behavior helps the child and other students. For example: "When you get in line quickly, it helps everyone have more time for recess."

To avoid giving a message that suggests pleasing you is what's most important, steer clear of phrases such as "I like," "I want," and "I appreciate." When a child is sensitive to being told what to do, he may feel manipulated if you use "I" statements.

Reinforcing Language in Action

If a situation like this happens	Try this (in private)
Jackson sometimes finds it hard to get along with certain classmates, but he goes out of his way to help Kevin.	"You made sure to help Kevin this morning and that made him feel valued. You were living out our rule to 'take care of each other.'"
Rihanna often balks at getting started on academic tasks, but she's excited about a math project and very engaged in it.	"Rihanna, I noticed that you got started on math right away. You already have two solutions that you can share with the class."
James usually struggles with transitions, but he leaves the classroom happily and starts his next task without complaint.	"Today, you lined up quickly and started art on time. What helped you make a smooth transition today?"

Share some responsibilities

Teachers who let children help make classroom decisions invite less defiance. These teachers send a clear message, not of compliance ("Do it because I say so"), but of community ("We're a team"). Some simple ways to do this are to seek students' advice about displays, give choices for read-aloud books, and provide options for certain assignments.

Why giving extra responsibility does NOT reward misbehavior

Some teachers have told me that they think giving children who act defiantly more responsibility rewards their "poor behavior." I understand this response.

Yet, our job as teachers is to help children learn to meet their needs in appropriate ways. What this looks and sounds like will differ from child to child.

Sometimes, the only way to help children who act defiantly is to give them choices and leadership responsibilities to clearly convey that they're important. This is not a reward. It's doing our job as teachers.

In addition to sharing some decision-making with students, give those who are prone to defiant behavior some extra responsibilities so they have more opportunities to feel significant. (See box above.) For example, if a child has difficulties with completing assignments, offer her more choices than you usually would. If transitions are challenging, give him a job to do: "Take this paperwork to the office. Then meet us in the gym for PE." If a child has a particular talent, give her a responsibility that lets her put that skill to use.

One year, a fifth grade student in a colleague's class frequently rebelled against accepting directions, but then the teacher and the student discovered a mutual interest in politics. During the presidential primary season that year, the teacher made it the student's job to find out the results and record them for the class. This one change didn't "fix" everything, but it was one of several steps my colleague tried that made a difference.

Teach how to disagree respectfully

It's empowering for all children—especially those who struggle with authority—to know that they may disagree with us. Allowing students to disagree doesn't mean accepting all forms of disagreement, of course.

Part of becoming a contributing member in a democratic society is learning how to disagree *respectfully*. Teaching students this skill is our responsibility as educators.

When teaching children appropriate ways to show disagreement, make it clear that in the moment, they still need to follow directions and rules. Let them know that later they can discuss what they think was unfair and what should be changed. You can use Interactive Modeling lessons (see pages 24–25) to teach children how they can show their disagreement in a respectful way. For example:

- using respectful words and phrases such as "I feel that," "I disagree with," and "I suggest"
- drawing a picture
- writing a letter or using the complaint box

For a list of children's books to help with this teaching, see pages 252–255.

Channel children's energy into positive directions

Children who challenge authority are often quite adept at taking on bigger causes of justice. Finding and working on an issue they view as important can help focus their energy and build their sense of significance. Offer them assignments such as writing letters to the school or town paper, exploring community service projects, or researching an environmental issue.

Adjust the rules

With some children, you may need to shift your expectations and give them more space or control than you might otherwise. Think about the tasks you absolutely need a child to do for his success and that of the class as a whole. Then think about tasks that you could let go of even though you think the child ideally should do them.

For instance, you may decide that the student must go along with transitions without complaint, but that you won't insist on as clean a desk for him as for other students. Or perhaps you decide that a student has to refrain from interrupting at whole-group time, but may move around during that time. If other children complain "that's not fair," remind them that it's your job to help everyone learn—and that this will look different for different students.

TEACHING TIP

Early Signs of Distress in Children

It may take a while to recognize specific warning signs for when a child is about to become defiant, but here are some typical ones:

- shifting in seat
- opening and closing fists
- drumming on desk with fists
- slumping shoulders
- crossing arms against chest
- having trouble making eye contact

Respond to warning signs early

Children who are defiant usually give clues that they're feeling distressed. If you watch for these early signs, you can often tell when they may be headed toward a confrontation.

Learn the child's triggers

After an incident has occurred, reflect on what happened leading up to it. Eventually, you'll begin to recognize what triggers a child's resistance (for example, an unexpected schedule change). Once you identify these triggers, plan what to do, such as diverting the child's attention, giving him some space, or taking other steps to de-escalate the situation.

Once you know what situations are likely to set off a child's defiance, share that information with the child. Together, plan how to manage these situations while maintaining self-control. Then share this plan with other teachers and staff who work with the child.

De-escalating Defiance

How to Respond Effectively in the Moment

The key to responding effectively to a child who's being defiant is to keep the child (and her classmates) safe while giving her a chance to cool down—so that she can again access her reasoning abilities.

When a child is behaving defiantly, avoid responses that will heighten her stress and invite more resistance. Simply put: don't push her buttons. In that moment, also don't expect that you can reason with the child or make an emotional appeal that will win her over to your side. Here are some more tips for responding effectively when a child is acting defiantly.

Avoid public confrontations

When you publicly give redirections or consequences to a student who's challenging you, the stakes become higher for both of you. You may feel compelled to assert your authority more forcefully than you would if you were dealing with the issue in private. Meanwhile, the student's goal may be to receive more attention, and the bigger the audience, the greater the attention.

So whenever possible, give reminders, redirections, and consequences privately. For example, move away from where the class is working and find a quiet spot to talk with the child.

Stay calm

When you notice that a child is getting upset or is refusing to do what you asked, tell yourself to slow down. Don't be in a rush to say or do anything (unless you need to take immediate action for safety's sake). If you stay calm, you give the child more of an opportunity to calm down, too.

Even if it feels personal, remember that what the child is doing ultimately has little to do with you. The child's goal is not to annoy, disrespect, or frustrate you, but to get his needs met. Allow yourself a few seconds to

pause or take a few slow, deep breaths. This will give you time to assess the situation calmly and objectively.

Respectfully remind or redirect

Students who have difficulty cooperating can be especially sensitive to being ordered around. When you respond to early warning signs or full-blown defiance, use respectful words and an even tone. If a child is beginning to show reluctance to make a transition, you might quietly say, "I know you don't like going to music class. Line up for now. We'll talk at the music room door." To a child who's challenging directions by standing up and yelling, you might say, "Andre, take a seat. You can read or draw for now." Remember to:

- Be brief. Avoid lectures and sarcasm.
- Speak in a calm, matter-of-fact tone.
- Use short, direct statements.
- Avoid questions (unless you will accept any answer).
- Keep your body language neutral.

Intervene as early as possible

Once you learn a child's triggers, respond with respectful reminders or redirections as soon as you see them. If you wait until a child has refused to do something, she will likely be less capable of responding rationally to your directions. The table on the next page gives some examples of these early interventions.

Early Interventions: Respectful Reminders and Redirections	
For a situation like this	**Try this**
You announce that it's cleanup time. Jason is tapping his pencil with his head down as he tries to finish his assignment. (Pencil tapping is often a sign of stress.)	**Redirect:** "Jason, you'll have time to finish this assignment later. I'm setting the timer for two minutes. Do your best to clean up. Then, meet us on the rug so you can show your classmates what you've done. Let me know if you need help."
Rachel interrupts a class discussion.	**Remind:** "Rachel, remember rug rules."
Robert has been sitting for a few minutes without starting his assignment. His shoulders are beginning to slump.	**Redirect:** "Robert, do you need help?" If yes, provide help. If no, follow up: "OK, I'll be back in two minutes to see what you have to say about ______."
Marianna is playing a math partner game with Shontee. She's losing and is beginning to look angry and question some of Shontee's moves.	**Remind:** "Marianna, do you want to keep playing with Shontee?" If yes, follow up: "Remind me how we practiced what to do when you and your partner disagree." If no, provide an alternative way to practice the math learning objective.

Offer limited choices if possible

Once a child has become defiant, you may decide to use consequences. However, because children who struggle with defiance are often seeking power, it can help to offer them two choices. By offering two options— not "do this"— you allow the child to hold on to her sense of significance while you remain consistent. This teaches the child and the class that she's still being held accountable for her behavior. The next page gives you some examples of offering limited choices.

Offering Choices for Logical Consequences	
If a situation like this happens	**Try this (in private)**
John refuses to do work despite your efforts to assist and make reasonable accommodations.	"John, you need to finish the assignment. You can do it at quiet time or during silent reading. Which will work for you?"
Anna refuses to move during a transition.	"Anna, you can either come with us now, or I can have [name of a colleague] come sit with you. Which do you choose?"
Ricky engages in rule-breaking behavior for which you would usually use time-out.	"Ricky, take a break. You can take your break in our take-a-break chair or in the spot you chose during our problem-solving conference."
Sara uses disrespectful words and body language while working with her group on a project.	"Sara, leave the group for now. You can do all of the assignment on your own, or you can do one part by yourself and then return to the group. We'll talk in a bit."

Avoid negotiating in the moment

Once you're in a situation in which a child has defied you, decide on a redirection or consequence (or the options of consequences offered to the child) and remain firm in your decision. Negotiating during the incident will invite further testing. It also sends the message that children can avoid a consequence or redirection by resisting.

If you ever find yourself in a power struggle, take a deep breath and disengage. Let the child (and the whole class, if watching) know that you're finished talking for now and will address the issue after the child calms down. For instance: "Max, we're done talking. Everyone else, get your writing journals and start on your stories from yesterday."

Give children time and space to cool down

Once children start to refuse directions or speak angrily to adults, they're likely in the "fight or flight" mindset. They feel agitated, their hearts pump faster, and they can't think rationally. Whenever possible, avoid any discussions, such as about reparations, until the child has completely calmed down.

This process may take longer than you think—possibly as much as a day. (Think about the last time you were really angry and how long you needed to calm down completely.) Also, consider ways to help the child regain self-control. Sometimes, gross motor movement, such as taking a walk or getting a drink, may help more than having the child sit still.

Once you've given a consequence or redirection, you need to watch to make sure the child follows it. But physically step back from the child and wait in silence to give her more space and lessen the sense that you're trying to control her. However, don't expect immediate compliance. A child who struggles following directions often needs a minute or two to decide what to do. If we insist on immediacy, she may automatically resist.

Reflect on what's working and what's not

Remember that your main goal in responding is to keep the child and other students safe. In-the-moment responses only play a limited role in helping children develop cooperation skills. Review pages 136–140 and continue using those proactive strategies. Think about whether the child needs more opportunities to practice a skill and build those opportunities into his daily schedule. Finding even a few minutes of extra practice time can help.

And take a step back to reflect: Are your expectations for yourself or the child simply too high? Is there another approach you haven't tried that might help?

If a Child Continues to Struggle With Defiance

No matter how skillfully you handle a situation, a child may still refuse to cooperate. Or the child may cooperate for a while, but then start to repeat acts of defiance. It's important not to consider your efforts a failure or think that the student is out to get you. There may be bigger issues at play for the child, or he may just need more time and practice learning certain behavior skills. Here are some more tips for follow up with these students.

Use a private signal

Consider agreeing on a private signal you both can use such as rubbing a hand on a cheek. When you give the signal to the student, you're telling her to do what you've just directed the whole class to do and that you'll check in with her as soon as you can.

When the child gives you the signal, it's an alert that she's getting frustrated. At this point, try to find ways to help the child before she becomes more upset. For example, consider having a brief, private meeting. You may also want to review the tips for responding in the moment on pages 141–145.

Have a back-up plan

If a child refuses to accept a consequence you have given, what's your Plan B? When appropriate, use the buddy teacher arrangement described on pages 34–35. The buddy teacher process lets the child know that consequences have meaning, but also gives him time to calm down and allows you to keep teaching.

Rather than engage with the child as you wait for the buddy teacher, continue teaching if it's safe to do so. However, if the child seems emotionally or physically agitated, stay close while sending the rest of the class to other areas of the room to work independently. When the child returns from the buddy room, remember to welcome him back. Once he's fully reentered classroom life, find a time to have a private check-in with him.

Practice giving consequences

If you have a child who's frequently resistant or really pushes your buttons, practice in advance the language and tone you'll use when delivering consequences. The more you practice, the more likely you'll remain calm, use respectful words, and decide on an appropriate consequence. It can be helpful to role-play with a colleague who can give you feedback on your delivery.

Invite the child's input

Sometimes it's helpful to ask the child to work with you to figure out how she can more readily cooperate in classroom life. I know this can feel uncomfortable at first, but if you absolutely must have a child's cooperation, one way to obtain it (and foster her sense of significance) is by holding a problem-solving conference.

In the conference, you first describe the child's behavior and why it's problematic for her and her classmates. Then explore with her why she's struggling with cooperation. Finally, you both agree on some strategies to try. To prepare for this discussion, think about:

- ***What you will say*** to highlight some positives you've noticed about the student or otherwise reestablish your rapport with her.
- ***How you will state the problem*** and its effects. For instance: "I've noticed that when I give directions for an activity you don't like, you often refuse to start. Sometimes that's a problem because you miss important learning opportunities or your classmates get distracted."
- ***What you will suggest*** about why the student might be resisting and how you will invite her input.
- ***What solutions you will propose.*** In preparing for these, think in terms of compromise. For instance, perhaps the child will agree to complete assignments without fuss, if she can work at an appropriate space of her choice or have some extra computer time. Or, perhaps you offer the child the chance to modify one assignment a day in exchange for her completing the others without objection.

Inviting students' input shows that you're willing to meet them halfway and builds their sense of significance. Remember, however, to do this during a calm time, not during or immediately after an incident. Trying to negotiate in the heat of the moment only invites more testing.

Try individual written agreements last

If you've tried multiple strategies and a student still has frequent episodes of defiance, an individual written agreement may help. This agreement gives the child a specific behavior goal on which to focus and feedback about how he's doing in meeting the goal. By breaking down being cooperative into specific behaviors and offering feedback whenever the child demonstrates those behaviors, the agreement can show him how to be successful and feel some control at school. Here's an example:

- ***Set a clearly defined goal.*** For example: "Luca will respectfully cooperate with directions and assignments." (While discussing the agreement, the teacher and Luca would brainstorm the specific behaviors that would constitute respectful cooperation, such as stopping when asked.)
- ***Use a reasonable standard for success*** in meeting the goal—"Luca will be successful eighty percent of the time."
- ***Have a way to track success*** that's easy for the student to see and understand—such as check marks on a chart.
- ***Set a nontangible reward*** for meeting the goal—"Every day Luca meets the goal, he can spend ten minutes with Mr. Foster setting up the next science experiments."

Consult with colleagues and specialists

Talk with other teachers about what you've tried and the results. They may be able to suggest other steps to take or point you toward other school resources, such as a school counselor, psychologist, or social worker.

How to Talk With Parents About Defiance

Some parents' experiences as students may color their reactions to news about their child's struggles with defiance. Parents who found the confines of school challenging may react defensively to reports that their child sometimes defies teachers. Be prepared to help these parents understand why defiance is problematic for their child (not you or the class) and how you're working to support him.

Other parents who have struggled with their children's defiance at home may be more open to what you have to share. These parents, however, may react punitively, which works against what you're trying to accomplish at school. Strive to help these parents understand that a punitive approach may exacerbate a child's struggles. Share how trying to proactively meet the child's needs instead can help (pages 136–140).

When talking with parents of children who often refuse to cooperate, begin by telling them about some positive behaviors you're noticing in their child. Then, when you get to a child's challenges, describe what you've observed using one or two concrete examples. Avoid judging, diagnosing, or labeling the child's difficulties. Instead, focus on the specific behavior and how it's interfering with learning. And be sure to invite the parents' ideas into your discussions.

Talking With Parents About Defiant Behavior

Instead of expressing frustration or judgment	Try naming specific behaviors and their impact on learning
"Suzi never follows directions. She just won't listen."	"Suzi often struggles following directions. For instance, last week I asked the class to clean their desks. Suzi said, 'My desk is the way I like it.' However, she has trouble finding things in her desk."
"Peter talks back and is very rude."	"When I give directions for assignments, Peter repeatedly questions them. I'm interested in your ideas about helping him get started on assignments more smoothly."
"Isabella needs to learn to do what she's told."	"Isabella needs to be able to voice her opinions, but she also needs to learn when it's appropriate to do so and when it's not. One thing we've been doing at school is . . ."
"If Eric keeps this up, no one is going to like him or want to be friends with him."	"I'm concerned that the behaviors I've described will hamper Eric's ability to make friends. I'd like to work with you to help him show classmates his positive qualities."

When children struggle with cooperation at school, the same is often true at home. If parents ask your advice on how to work with their child, you may want to share some general tips like these:

- ***Give the child some choices*** and power at home. Choose which issues are nonnegotiables, such as being ready for school on time, and which ones can have some flexibility, such as when to do homework.
- ***Keep calm in moments of defiance.*** Speak softly and in a matter-of-fact tone. Use words that invite cooperation rather than demand compliance. For example, "Homework needs to be done before 7:15. You can do it first or play first. What's your plan?"
- ***When the child is calm,*** discuss a "cooling off" spot and strategies he can use to calm down there.

If parents want to read up on issues of defiance, share the resources on pages 256–260. You might also suggest that they read children's books with their child—see pages 252–255 for some useful titles.

Closing Thoughts

When dealing with children who struggle with cooperation, think in terms of their need to feel significant and how you can provide opportunities for them to meet that need. It's not easy to work with students who challenge authority, but if you persevere, you'll likely start to see progress. Recognize and reinforce their steps in choosing cooperation over defiance. Children will learn that there are more productive ways to feel significant than by defying adults.

Key Points

Remember not to take it personally when children refuse to cooperate. Instead, remind yourself that they're likely trying to feel significant.

To promote cooperation, use proactive strategies, such as finding ways to help the child feel more in control and have some power.

Respond calmly and offer limited choices, if possible, during acts of defiance.

Focus on the positives, not just the challenges, when talking with parents about their child's struggles to cooperate, and invite their input.

6

Disengagement

Disengagement

Reaching Children Who Appear Unmotivated

School's so boring. All of us find certain tasks uninspiring at one time or another. But for some students, nearly everything seems uninspiring. They simply do not show much, if any, interest in *anything* having to do with school and yet there is no known disability or barrier getting in their way of learning. Other students may be engaged in certain areas of school (perhaps art and music), but not in others, such as math.

Students who struggle with motivation often express their disenchantment throughout the day. During class discussions, they may look bored, talk to friends, or ask unrelated questions ("What time is recess?"). Presented with a writing assignment, they might stare at the piece of paper, fiddle with the pencil, or go to the bathroom for a long time.

When math time rolls around they may complain, "Why do I need to learn this?" And when they do hand in work, it's often done as quickly as possible and well below the quality we know they're capable of producing.

It's all too easy to get frustrated by students who are disengaged or unmotivated, especially after we've worked hard to plan engaging lessons. We may feel personally affronted and want to respond by saying "I'll make you do this assignment! You can miss every recess until you get it done!"

Of course, in our calmer moments, we know that we can't make children do anything or force them to become motivated. But we also can't give up on them. Their futures depend on our helping them connect to and become excited about their learning. The good news is that there's a lot we can do to support them in developing internal motivation.

In this chapter, you'll learn some common reasons why students appear unmotivated, how to help most students discover more passion for school, what to do in the moment when a student chooses not to do an assignment due to lack of motivation, and practical advice for talking sensitively with parents about children who seem disengaged at school.

Why Do Children Become Unmotivated?

One reason high school students give for dropping out of school is that they're bored. Although your students may seem a long way off from giving up on school, the unfortunate reality is that many elementary school students are already starting to feel disconnected from school. So they disengage from their learning and stop caring about school.

Children's feelings of boredom are red flags for us teachers that their needs aren't being met or that they lack skills essential for school success.

Schoolwork doesn't seem important

Some children don't see how schoolwork matters to their lives. As a result, completing assignments often does not give them the same sense of accomplishment as it does for other students. For some students, not having any choice in what or how they learn can also sap their motivation.

Need for significance

Some children fear making mistakes or failing tests, quizzes, or other assignments. They may feel that if they don't succeed at every school task, they'll seem less competent and important. To avoid this negative outcome, these children try to avoid, often at all costs, any task that might prove challenging or pose a risk of failing.

Need for fun

For still other students, their need for fun underlies their disengagement. They just don't find the schoolwork they're being asked to do interesting or engaging. As a result, they look for other ways to meet this emotional need—by doing anything other than their schoolwork!

Need for belonging

At times, children try to fit in with peers who are disengaged or who actively look down on any school-related tasks. To meet their sense of belonging, these children suppress their own interests and feelings and try to show that they're just like these classmates. By appearing not to care about school, they hope to solidify friendships or make new friends with students who act "too cool for school."

Lack of skills

Some children simply have not developed the skills required to motivate themselves when tasks are challenging or uninteresting. They may not have had much practice in figuring out what interests them, how to work independently, or how to get unstuck if they face a challenge.

Still other children lack academic skills. They've come to find school so challenging and have felt so unsuccessful that they've given up. They start to believe that they're not capable of the work and so they refuse to try.

Motivation and child development

Curiosity and a desire to learn are hallmarks of childhood. However, some children struggle with a lack of interest or motivation at certain ages because of what might be happening developmentally.

Some Child Development Characteristics Related to Lack of Engagement or Motivation

Grade	Characteristic	Influences on engagement
2nd (ages 6–8)	• Don't like taking risks or making mistakes • Sometimes inward-looking and moody • Very concerned about finished product	• May avoid assignments for fear of making mistakes • View certain tasks or assignments as impossible and quickly give up on them
4th (ages 8–10)	• Complain frequently • Critical of self and others, including adults • Often worried or anxious • Can be sullen, moody, and negative	• May find fault with assignments or be skeptical of why they should do them • May worry about making mistakes on assignments and thus avoid them • Question teacher's authority to give assignments or whether assignments are meaningful or relevant
6th (ages 10–12)	• Can be inward-looking and moody • Like to challenge rules and test limits • Enjoy arguing and debating • Worry about who's "in" and who's "out"	• Want to see what will happen if they refuse to do certain work • Trying to connect socially with classmates who, at least outwardly, view academics negatively

You may encounter students at any grade or age who lack motivation. But if you teach at the grade levels listed in the table, be especially alert for how developmental characteristics might be further diminishing students' engagement.

We can never be one hundred percent sure why a child is bored, disengaged, or unmotivated. However, by exploring the likely causes and teaching them positive ways to meet their needs, we'll be better able to help them build stronger connections to school and their learning.

Fostering Engagement

Proactive Steps to Promote Students' Motivation

The goal in working with students who seem bored is to build their internal sense of curiosity and drive to succeed. Beware of using extrinsic motivators like rewards. Rewards might get children to complete assignments in the short term and may be an appropriate last resort, but for most children, rewards will do little to resolve any issues in the long term.

Some children will need guidance to learn how to motivate themselves; to understand what it looks, sounds, and feels like to be fully engaged; or even to figure out what truly interests them. Here are some proactive steps to take to help students in these areas.

Build strong relationships with students

When students feel appreciated by their teachers, they tend to find school more engaging and thus are naturally motivated to perform. They're more open to attempting assignments that might not appeal to them or that seem too difficult at first. And when teachers know what excites their students, they can more easily adapt assignments for them.

Talk with students and find out what their lives are like outside of school, what interests they have, and what talents they want to develop. When you have trusting relationships with students, it's easier to create a culture in which learning is "cool."

Foster a growth mindset

Strive to instill in all students what researcher Carol Dweck calls a "growth mindset"—a belief that we can all change with effort and that mistakes aren't a reflection of inner worth, but merely setbacks we can learn to overcome. One way to do this is to create a safe learning environment. For example, honor risk-taking as part of learning. Give children open-ended questions and assignments and then highlight the benefits of the wide range of responses and products they come up with.

When children make mistakes, respond in ways that encourage problem-solving. For instance: "You did make some spelling errors. What are some ways you could work on correcting those? What might you do differently next time?" Use children's literature, biographies, and events from history to highlight the positive role mistakes can play in life.

Give children positive feedback for their efforts to learn, not just for successful end products. Also, post works in progress from students of varying abilities, not just examples of completed products or the "best" work. In classrooms where learning is viewed as a process and growth mindsets are fostered, children are much less likely to avoid work because they fear making mistakes or failing and more likely to take academic risks.

Reinforce students' efforts to motivate themselves

Offer students positive feedback (in private) when they take on challenging or unengaging tasks. Follow up with a question to help them reflect on how they overcame a challenge and motivated themselves to stay on track. When you reinforce students' progress and effort, no matter how small it might seem (to you or them), you give them something to build on.

Reinforcing Language in Action	
If something like this happens	**Try this**
A student quickly and efficiently completes a test prep practice sheet for the first time.	"Faustino, you finished that page quickly and carefully. What helped you do that?"
A student who ordinarily does the minimum goes above and beyond the requirements for a research project. This student discovers a great deal about the country she chose to study.	"Kiri, it was fascinating to read everything you discovered about India! You found out so much. What do you think of your research results? What helped you to reach them?"
A student who often writes very little during writing workshop comes up with an interesting and detailed draft for a persuasive essay.	"Tomas! You have a knack for persuading people. These two arguments convinced me that I should spend less time on my cell phone and laptop! What do you think of your essay?"

Take a second look at lessons

When learning is interactive and purposeful to children, they're more likely to be invested and less likely to deem those who excel or like school as "uncool." Design student-centered lessons so that they captivate and hold students' attention. For example, try to choose topics of special interest to your students. And even when you have no say over the topic, try to find real-life connections that might draw students in. Here are some more tips:

- ***Offer choices when possible.*** When students have a choice as to what to study or how to accomplish a task, they're often more committed to their work. Choices can be simple. For instance, children can choose what book to read independently or what topic to write about. Or, you could offer them a choice of how to practice a certain skill, such as studying spelling words using flashcards or by highlighting and working on the "tricky" parts.

Choices can also be more complex. For example, children might select a topic for a research study and then plan how to present what they discover. Choices at this level can lead to deeper involvement, as students discover what interests them, work more at their own pace, and develop greater expertise and skills.

➤ ***Share learning goals.*** Before jumping into a new unit, lesson, or assignment, briefly explain the learning goals. If possible, tie goals into the bigger picture of life outside of school and make connections to their world. It may be obvious to us why learning a given skill is important, but it's not always as clear to our students.

Another way to make learning meaningful is to help students connect it to what they already know. Try beginning a lesson by asking students to share prior knowledge or experiences to help build their investment and interest.

TEACHING TIP

Help Students Discover Their Passions

To help all children discover their interests:

- Provide a wide variety of books, assignments, and projects.
- Point out when a student seems to be particularly excited about a topic.
- Meet with them individually to support their efforts to explore areas of possible interest.

➤ ***Give students a chance to work with others.*** Students' need for belonging can be very motivating. As you plan assignments, think about how to structure some so that students have opportunities to work with others.

For example, give students a few minutes to talk with a partner about questions related to a topic before launching a whole-group discussion. Or, pair students up to do a partner reading, math assignment, science investigation, or social studies research project. When a child knows that his contribution is vital to his group or partner's performance, he's much more likely to rise to the occasion.

Teach children to evaluate their own work

Sometimes children simply do not understand what it takes to do a thorough job on an assignment. They may work perfunctorily and then ask, "Is this enough?" because they're trying to figure out what the expectations are. Provide these children with rubrics and clear guidelines so that they can learn to judge for themselves how they've done on a given assignment.

Teach children how to "unbore" themselves

Not every assignment will appeal to every child, and some may seem routine, even dull. To help students discover how to persevere and make tasks more engaging for themselves:

- ***Brainstorm how to approach assignments*** they don't find appealing initially. Students can have a great deal of insight into what would make an assignment more engaging—and students are very likely to be pulled in by their classmates' ideas.
- ***Model what it looks like*** to create a personal challenge for an assignment—for instance, by doing it within a certain length of time, with only a certain number of errors, or in some creative way.
- ***Discuss examples*** of people who spend hours practicing their craft (athletes, musicians, scientists). Often the tasks students find less exciting are those that require repetition, so knowing the value of regular practice can help students develop perseverance.

Be cautious in assessing motivation

Students may outwardly appear disengaged when they are, in fact, deeply interested in what we're teaching. This apparent disconnect between what students show us and what they're actually thinking is especially common in children who are more introverted. Spend some time observing and talking with a student before reaching a conclusion about her motivational level.

On the next page, you can see some ways to tell that a student is engaged even if she doesn't participate actively in group discussions.

- In one-on-one conversations, the child shows excitement about what you've been teaching.
- The child's parents comment on something the child has told them about what she's been learning.
- The child easily begins assignments and stays focused on them.

Consider other factors

Some children who have learning challenges may seem disengaged or unmotivated. Because of these challenges, a child may have a harder time taking in information, completing assigned tasks, or keeping up with the pace of schoolwork. Work with specialists at your school to rule out such possibilities before deciding that the problem is one of motivation.

Engaging the Disengaged

How to Respond Effectively in the Moment

When you encounter students who appear uninterested or struggle to start assignments, remember that teacher-imposed consequences won't lead to internal motivation. In situations such as these, the goal is to respond in ways that help children look within and discover what will engage them. Here are some guidelines for responding when children seem disengaged.

Intervene early

When possible, intervene as soon as you notice a student appearing to day-dream or otherwise having difficulty starting an assignment. By checking in with a student at the beginning of assignments, you'll be more likely to figure out what the roadblock is and how best to help her overcome it. For example, the student might need you to break the task into smaller steps, so it feels more manageable to her.

The longer the child goes without doing any work, the further behind she falls. Then, at some point, the work can seem insurmountable. The table on the next page gives some examples of what you might say (in private) to students who are struggling to begin assignments.

Helping Children Get Started	
If something like this happens	**Try this**
During writing workshop time, you notice that Alex has not written anything for five minutes.	"Alex, what are you planning to write about today? How did you want to start?" OR "Alex, what have you been thinking about so far? Let me take some notes while you talk." (Leave the notes with the student.)
Anju complains about a math assignment: "Why do I need to know this? This is so boring."	"Anju, would you like to hear some ways people in real life use what we're learning today?" OR "Anju, do you remember when we talked about how to unbore ourselves? Which strategy for self-motivation can you use for math today?"
During a lesson in which students have a choice of how to complete a task, Aliyah (one of the most capable students in the class) chooses the least challenging option.	"I'm curious about why you chose Option D, Aliyah. Tell me more about how you think it will help you learn about this topic."

Provide a choice for completing the assignment

When a student has failed to complete an assignment, it can be tempting to take a punitive approach, such as requiring him to stay in from recess to do the work. Avoid giving in to this temptation. For many children, recess is the only time they can engage in active play that's essential for their growth.

Instead, offer the student a choice about when to complete unfinished work. For example: "You have to finish your research work from today. You can either do it by having a working lunch or by coming into school early tomorrow. Which do you choose?" This sends the message that the work has to be completed while involving the student in deciding when.

Use a matter-of-fact tone and positive language

Faced with students who refuse to do assignments, teachers sometimes use language that is adversarial, which can compound students' struggles. For instance, by saying "You wasted your work time, so now you owe me your free time," teachers inadvertently create a me-versus-you dynamic. This approach can result in a power struggle with the student digging in her heels.

Instead, try a let's-work-together approach: "I noticed you were having difficulty finishing your math. The project needs to be completed by tomorrow. What do you need to help you reach that goal?" This table provides more examples of using positive teacher language with a matter-of-fact tone.

Instead of	Try
"If you'd just put a little more effort in, you could be great at math."	"I know you can do this math assignment. How can I help?"
"You didn't finish anything during writing time! Everyone else did their work then, so you can just do yours at recess."	"The goal for writing time today was to draft the setting for your story. What's your plan for doing that so your partner can help you revise it tomorrow?"
"You haven't even started yet! What have you been doing?"	"Kendall, our work time will last about thirty minutes. Ten minutes has already passed. Let's create a plan for making good use of the next twenty minutes."

These in-the-moment responses can help shape students' short-term motivation, but a broader approach is necessary for lasting effects. Keep seeking to understand the reasons for students' struggles with motivation, strengthening your relationships with students, and using the other proactive strategies from pages 157–162.

If a Child Continues to Struggle

If students continue to have difficulties getting started on assignments, finishing their work, or doing their best, try these next steps:

Reinforce efforts to persevere

No matter how engaging we make our lessons and assignments, some students may still find certain tasks boring. Revisit the proactive strategies and adjust one or two to reteach these students. When you do see students persevere and complete tasks they ordinarily find boring or difficult, be sure to give positive feedback. Share this news with parents. (See pages 168–170 for more on communicating with parents about issues related to motivation.)

Strategize with students, not for them

As teachers, we often spend a great deal of time thinking about how to inspire students who act disengaged—and those students are more than happy to leave the job to us. My colleague Mike Anderson told me of a fifth grade student who regularly struggled to complete her homework. After spending most of the year devising different solutions for her, Mike finally realized that by taking on all the problem-solving, he was not helping the student address her homework challenge or develop intrinsic motivation.

It wasn't until Mike shared problem-solving responsibilities with the student that the situation improved. So, invite your student into the conversation and explore why she's struggling and how you can both find solutions. One way to do this is by using a problem-solving conference. To plan for this conference, think about:

- ***How you will positively reinforce what the student is doing well.*** This will help set a positive tone for the conversation.

- ***How to state the problem and its impact.*** For example: "I've noticed that at writing time, you often have a hard time figuring out what to write about and getting started. You also frequently say that writing is boring."
- ***Possible causes of the problem.*** If the child is at a loss as to what's causing her lack of engagement, name some possible reasons and be open to reasons she suggests.
- ***Strategies to help the child motivate herself.*** For example, you might suggest that the child brainstorm with you topics that might be more interesting, periodically share progress on a piece of writing with a student from an upper grade, or have a target amount of writing to do per day. The child may also have ideas about what would help her, so be open to other options, too.

Seek help from colleagues

Sometimes a trusted colleague can shed light on what's happening with a student who appears unmotivated or suggest other ways to help. Invite a colleague to observe a student during a work time that's typically challenging. Or, share what you know and what you've tried. Together, brainstorm what may be going on for the child and what you might do differently.

Try individual written agreements last

Some students become so stuck in a pattern of disengagement that you may need to try an individual written agreement. This agreement gives the child specific behavior goals to accomplish and frequent feedback about whether she's meeting those goals. It can let you both see that she can indeed improve in this area. Here's an example of how an agreement might look and sound in the context of disengagement:

- ***Set a clearly defined goal.*** For example: "Lin will get started on assignments quickly and spend the designated work time focused on them." (During a conversation about the agreement, the teacher and Lin would flesh out in more detail exactly how this will look—for instance, staying in one spot and asking questions only when help is needed).

- ***Use a reasonable standard for success*** in meeting the goal—"Lin will be successful seventy-five percent of the time."
- ***Have a way to track success*** that's easy for the student to see and understand—check marks on a chart or craft sticks in a jar, for example.
- ***Have a nontangible reward*** for meeting the goal—"If Lin meets the goal, she can work on a special technology project of her choice."

About Homework Struggles

If students struggle to complete in-school assignments, they'll often struggle with homework as well. Here are some tips to help make homework successful for all students, especially those who are challenged by it:

- ***Make homework as meaningful as possible.*** As with schoolwork, children are more motivated to complete homework when they find it purposeful. Here are two ideas to try:

  1) Include a brief note about the purpose(s) of a given assignment.

  2) Have students do something related to their homework during school the following day. For instance, students could meet in groups to discuss a reading assignment, or compare data they collected at home with a partner.

- ***Limit the amount of homework required.*** When creating homework assignments, consider where children are developmentally and their need for play, rest, and family time.
- ***Involve the child in discussions with parents about homework.*** Parents and teachers generally work on a child's struggles with homework without consulting the child. When children are brought into these conversations, they're more likely to be invested in the solutions.

- ***Steer clear of using consequences for uncompleted homework.*** Because we have no way of knowing if a child truly has the time and support at home to do assignments, it's not appropriate to give students consequences for not doing homework.

For additional resources on how to make homework more meaningful for students, search on "homework" at www.responsiveclassroom.org.

How to Talk With Parents About Lack of Motivation

When approached sensitively, parents often have a great deal of insight to offer about their children's disengagement. Perhaps they'll tell you that their child has always been worried about making mistakes. Or parents might share a past experience or recent event that's led to difficulties in a particular subject area. In addition, many parents are willing to offer ideas about how to help get their child engaged in learning.

The challenge, as always, is to share a child's struggles without judgment and to be as open as possible to parents' observations and ideas. Avoid labels such as "lazy," "careless," "lacks focus, or "not interested in school." Instead, describe what you have observed in an objective way and explain the efforts you've taken to increase the child's investment and participation.

Prepare for these conversations

Try to anticipate what parents might say and how you can respond empathetically. Ask open-ended questions to explore the parents' views of their child's struggles. Then, be ready to describe what you have been trying and why. The table on the next page gives some ways to get these conversations started.

Talking With Parents About Lack of Motivation	
Instead of this	**Try this**
"Nick just doesn't get much work done. Does he have trouble with motivation at home, too?"	"Nick sometimes struggles with starting and finishing his assignments. I'd like to see him be more engaged with his work. I'll share what I've been trying and I'd also like to hear any ideas you have."
"I have been working so hard to get Andrea to care more about her work. She does the bare minimum—just enough to get by."	"When Andrea is interested, her work really shows her talents. For instance, her poems were very moving. Often, however, she works too fast and doesn't reach that same level of quality. When we researched a famous leader, she found two facts right away, and then said she was done. How does this compare with what you experience at home?"
"At school, Lana seems to just want to socialize and hang out. Schoolwork really doesn't interest her."	"I'm hoping to share with you what we've been doing to help Lana be as excited about the academic parts of our day as she is about the social aspects."

Anticipate parents' reactions

Here are two common parental reactions and how you might respond:

- ***If parents want a quick fix.*** Some parents may have been concerned about their child's lack of motivation for a while. They may be relieved to hear you recognize this, but they may also want to find solutions right away, such as external motivators. Share with these parents the fact that external motivators do little to help most children in the long run, and let them know what you're doing to address the behavior.

➤ ***If parents are surprised.*** Other parents may be surprised about their child's lack of engagement, especially if the child appears self-motivated at home. Discuss with them what might be happening with their child at school. Listen carefully to what they share about their child's home experiences. These details may provide key insights for ways to help the child feel more motivated at school.

For all parents, help them keep in mind that developing motivation may take some time, even with the support of caring adults at home and in school. As always, be open to what parents share with you. You may also want to tell them about the proactive steps from pages 157–162 that they could try at home.

Closing Thoughts

Helping children learn how to motivate themselves can be some of the most challenging work we do as teachers. Yet, the rewards of that work are great. Helping a child discover the joy of learning is an accomplishment rarely to be rivaled in teaching. It's so heartening to see a child who has previously shown no interest in any subject light up over an assignment or put his all into a project. Although you may encounter some bumps along the way, your efforts can help children reach deep within themselves and become more invested in—and excited about—their schoolwork.

Key Points

- Use proactive strategies to help children become engaged and motivated, such as by offering choices and designing lessons that build on their interests and abilities.
- Respond as soon as you see a child struggling to start or complete an assignment. Use a matter-of-fact tone and positive teacher language.
- Let parents know what you're doing to help students become more motivated. Work with parents to find out any information that might help, such as what excites their child outside of school.

7

Sillness and Showing Off

Silliness and Showing Off

Helping Children Focus on Learning

I once heard a story about the comic Jim Carrey that went like this: When he was in school, a teacher responded to his frequent jokes in class by making a deal with him. If he could focus on his work, she'd give him fifteen minutes at the end of the day to do "stand-up" in front of his classmates. Carrey said it was one of the few years in school when he was able to focus on academics.

The story always stuck with me, even more so when I heard that my colleague Mike Anderson used a similar strategy with fifth graders. Many of his students became quite silly during math, making a funny comment or joke and causing their classmates to roar with laughter. Mike took many proactive steps to address the problem—talking one-on-one with students, practicing what to do when someone else became silly, and holding class meetings. But the problem persisted. During one discussion, he and the students came up with a strategy like that of Jim Carrey's teacher. Mike gave students a brief "comedy slot" on Wednesday afternoons during which they could tell jokes and be silly. But at math time, the jokes had to stop. Later, he told me that having those few minutes on Wednesday seemed to satisfy his students and their math focus dramatically increased (even when the jokes weren't that funny).

Of course, this strategy won't work for every child or every class, but it gets at a central issue: silliness and showing off are behaviors that meet real needs. And if students aren't given an outlet for meeting these needs, they'll find their own.

In this chapter, you'll learn more about these needs, strategies for teaching children appropriate ways to meet them, ways to respond to silliness (without encouraging more of it), and tips for discussing the issue with parents.

Why Do Children Act Silly or Show Off?

Sometimes, we forget that the children we teach are just that—children. Humor, silliness, playfulness, and showing off are hallmarks of childhood, and we should expect to experience some at every grade.

Just for the fun of it

Children often act silly or show off because these are ways to have fun. They literally need to giggle with friends over something silly that happened, make funny faces that crack everyone up, or tell jokes. Knock-knock jokes in younger grades grow into puns in the middle grades which, in turn, give rise to jokes with innuendo by sixth grade. Although what children find funny changes, most love humorous poems, songs, books, and movies throughout childhood.

For a sense of belonging

Joking and showing off also help children connect to those around them. Children who laugh together feel close to one another, even if only for a moment. For some students, a shared moment of laughter can lead to close friendships. Humor, whimsy, and entertaining others are powerful ways that children get to know each other and solidify their sense of belonging.

For a sense of significance

Showing off and telling jokes are also ways children gain a sense of importance. Some children may only feel special when they're the center of attention. Being a little more dramatic, a little funnier, or a little more "wild and crazy" is a way for these students to stand out from the crowd.

Silliness, showing off, and child development

Although silliness and showing off appear in every grade, they tend to be more pronounced in first, third, and fifth grades, times when most children are experiencing intensive growth in social areas. In the grades where children tend to be consolidating social growth—second, fourth, and sixth grades—students might actually need their teachers to bring out their humor and help relieve some of the pressure they put on themselves.

Some Child Development Characteristics Related to Silliness and Showing Off

Grade	Characteristic	Influence on silliness and showing off
1st (ages 5–7)	• Love jokes, riddles, guessing games • Active; need to move a great deal • Concerned with social issues • Very verbal; very social	• Need an audience to try out new jokes and humor • Want to impress certain classmates • May need more frequent social outlets than currently provided
3rd (ages 7–9)	• Tire easily • Need to move a lot • Very social; concerned with social issues • Very verbal; like to explain things	• Need more chances to move • Are more concerned with social issues than academics • Need to process what they're learning by talking

CONTINUED ON PAGE 176

Grade	Characteristic	Influence on silliness and showing off
5th (ages 9–11)	• Very social • Often expressive and talkative	• May need to joke and use humor to explain thinking • Want to maintain and develop friendships through joking or exaggerating personal strengths

Naturally, children in every grade sometimes make ill-timed jokes, lose themselves in silliness, and show off too much. It takes children time to develop their comedic timing and ability to share center stage. With your guidance, they can learn to channel their natural desire for fun into productive (and still enjoyable) learning.

Balancing Silliness With Seriousness

Proactive steps to promote productive playfulness

Providing children with productive ways to meet their needs for silliness and performing will go a long way toward preventing them from meeting those needs in other ways. For instance, if they don't have opportunities to be silly, the giggles may come out just when you want them to be most attentive. What follows are some guidelines for encouraging an appropriate balance of fun and seriousness to enhance children's social-emotional and academic growth.

Give some silly time

Consider these ideas for ways to meet children's needs for playfulness and learning:

➤ ***Add to the classroom library.*** Stock it with humor-based books that children can explore. As you choose books for read-alouds, consider children's developmental needs. For example, Louis Sachar's *Sideways Stories from Wayside School* usually meet first graders' silly needs; Jack Gantos's books often do the same for older students.

- ***Include fun games and energizers.*** Look for light-hearted games like Do You Love Me, Honey? or What Are You Doing? to play at morning meetings or closing circles. Consider using brief energizers to break up the daily routine and make it easier for children to focus in on the next lesson or task.
- ***Build humor into academic lessons.*** For example, look for books and articles that reveal the humor in historical or scientific events. Or, design tasks that tap into children's playful side. Instead of having students write a report, give them a choice of doing an interview or infomercial. For an insect unit, I let students create their own insects. Their creations had to be scientifically accurate, but students were free to imagine unique ways their insects might use body parts.
- ***Give children the occasional spotlight.*** Use Readers' Theater or dramatic interpretations of stories to allow children to be the center of attention. Do dramatic readings of poems, sing songs, play games with a dramatic element, and let those who like to perform shine in similar, productive ways.

For a list of children's books, see pages 252–255; for resources on energizers and fun games, see pages 256–260.

Teach how to stop and refocus

Children need help learning to regulate their emotions. Model what it looks and sounds like to laugh about something funny for a few seconds and then to stop and refocus. For instance, after everyone laughs at something, you might say, "Oh, that was funny. Now, I'm going to take a few deep breaths to get myself focused back onto our discussion." Sometimes, I would even go to our take-a-break spot to show how that helped me to regroup.

Signal when shifting gears

Children are better able to refocus on academics when you provide a quick transition from fun to work. If, instead, you go right back into academics, it can feel jarring to them, and they may continue with the joking. After a funny incident, use a signal, such as a raised hand to show "Stop," to alert students when it's time to transition back to learning. You might also want to say, "OK, let's get back to ______" or "Now it's time to return to our lesson. Who can remind us of our goal for this lesson?"

Establish expectations for seriousness

Use class rules as the starting point for a conversation about behavior expectations for instructional and work times, and why these are important. Model what it looks and sounds like to listen, stay on topic during discussions and partner chats, and focus on independent work tasks. You may also want to teach children creative ways to show appreciation (such as silent clapping or another nonverbal signal) rather than whooping it up.

As you strive to help children live out these expectations, be consistent in your response to jokes, silly comments, and playful antics. It's confusing if a child's fooling around is acceptable one day, but a similar behavior receives a consequence on another.

> TEACHING TIP
>
> **Avoid Overdoing Humorous Activities**
>
> While it's important to read humorous poetry and be playful with students, it's also important to know when not to do such activities. If students are on the verge of the giggles, try doing calming activities, such as a silent version of Simon Says or a peaceful song.

Be mindful of your own silliness

Because we usually have center stage, it's easy for us to overdo humor, especially when students enjoy our antics. Of course we want to be natural and playful. When we are, it helps children relax, improves our relationships with them, and makes learning more enjoyable. However, we can go too far. Sometimes when I got too silly, my students responded in kind and it was hard to get them back on track. Also, if we're frequently joking or going into "actor" mode, but rarely allowing children to do the same, they may try to compete with us or resent us for being unfair.

Teach how to keep the sillies away

To help them keep their focus on learning, teach children respectful ways of responding when someone is trying to make them laugh. Use Interactive Modeling and role-play to demonstrate responses such as ignoring the behavior, moving away, or respectfully telling the person to stop (for example, "That's funny. I need to concentrate on my work now. Maybe we can trade jokes during lunch."). For more information on Interactive Modeling and role-play, see pages 24–25.

Reinforce students' efforts at regulating themselves

Managing one's emotions is a skill that takes children time and practice to develop. When you take time to reinforce students' efforts at exercising this skill, you'll help them solidify it. Remember to name specifically what they did that was helpful.

Reinforcing Language in Action

If a situation like this happens	Try this
Your class often has a hard time regrouping after something funny happens. Today, a poster fell down while you were teaching. Students laughed, but quickly refocused when you said it was time to return to the lesson.	"Wow! Look at how fast you have your voices off and your eyes back on me. You're learning how to regroup after something funny happens."
Two students usually giggle for a long time when their classmate Doris makes funny noises. Today, Doris tries to engage them in her silliness, but they stay on task.	Privately (after Doris goes to the time-out spot): "Tonya and Denise, even though Doris tried to make you laugh, you stuck with your stories. I can't wait for you to share what you wrote."
Michael frequently makes comments using movie lines. Today, he makes such a comment. You use a private signal to alert him that this isn't the time for these (see page 146 for more on these signals). Michael refrains from making another comment during the lesson.	Privately: "Michael, our signal seems to be working. I signaled after you quoted from *Star Wars* and you held off making any more comments. What strategy did you use to stay focused on our lesson today?"

Calming the Silliness

How to Respond Effectively in the Moment

Even with our best proactive work, children will occasionally struggle with silliness and showing off. It's also challenging for children to regulate themselves if someone near them is laughing or being goofy. As children learn how to stay focused and ignore distractions, they're bound to make mistakes and get caught up in the moment. When that happens, here are some tips for bringing the silliness to an end and helping children refocus on learning.

Respond early

As you get to know your students better, you'll be able to detect some signs that children's willpower is diminishing. The sooner you respond, the sooner children can regain self-control in most situations. If you wait until a fit of giggling has set in, children will have a much harder time recovering. When you respond early, you're also more likely to get children back on track quickly—with just a few words or a nonverbal cue, such as eye contact. The more timely—and "smaller"—your response, the less interruption to learning there will be.

Respond respectfully and minimally

When you respond, be respectful, but refrain from giving the child too much attention, which can provoke more silliness. For example, if you respond with a lecture, sarcasm, or "What's so funny?" you can make the situation worse. Instead, remind or redirect children with mater-of-fact language, using as few words as possible.

Reminding and Redirecting Language in Action	
If a situation like this happens	**Try this**
During a science lesson on the planets, you say the word "Uranus," and most of your class bursts out laughing.	**Redirect:** "Now that we have that out of our system, eyes up here, voices off, hands in laps. Take a deep breath." Pause so that students can regroup and then start back into your lesson.
Your class has an inside joke about the word "hobnob." When someone says it, everyone laughs. However, students have agreed to use the word for fun only during snack, lunch, and recess. Today, Jaime says "hobnob" during a lesson, and many children begin to snicker.	**Redirect and remind:** "Stop. Show me what we agreed to do." Make eye contact and wait for students to follow through with their agreement.
Lila and Frankie are partners for a math game. You notice that they're starting to get giggly and lose focus.	**Remind and move closer to them:** "Lila, Frankie, show me how to have fun and still focus on math. I'll watch." Stay for a few minutes until they seem to be back in control.

Use logical consequences

If you respond early, your reminder or redirection will often be enough to help a child shift gears and return to a learning mindset. At other times, a logical consequence may be more effective. Perhaps you missed the early signs or the child has lost too much self-control. Or from what you know about the child, your teacher instincts tell you that a redirection at this point will likely not help. In situations like these, use a reasonable logical consequence.

Logical Consequences in Action	
If a situation like this happens	**Try this**
Lila and Frankie are partners for a math game. When they first started to get silly, you moved close to them and helped them get back on track. Just a few minutes later, they're throwing cards at each other and laughing loudly.	**Use loss of privilege:** • "I'm giving you each a new partner," or • "You each need to play the game on your own. Take turns against yourself." **Follow up with each child later** (because of how disruptive their behavior was): "What was going on for you during the card game? Do you know why you lost the privilege of playing together? What could you do differently next time?"
Instead of "hobnob," Jaime keeps trying other humorous words to get the class to laugh.	**Use time-out:** "Jaime, take a break."
During a math lesson, you direct students to partner chat about how they came up with their answers. While you check in with two students, you hear Kim and Mary singing a pop song and giggling instead of talking about their work.	**Use time-out:** "Kim and Mary, each of you needs to take a break." **Follow up with each girl later** (because of how off task they were): "What was going on for you? Do you know why I sent you to time-out? What's something that would help you follow our rules next time?"

In addition to responding in the moment, keep evaluating why a particular child or your class may be struggling with silliness or showing off. Continue using the proactive strategies outlined on pages 176–179, adapting them according to the individual child and situation.

If a Child Continues to Act Silly

If some students continue to struggle with too much clowning around or ill-timed jokes, you may need to supplement your use of proactive and reactive strategies. Try some of these ideas to provide additional support for these students.

Hold a class discussion

If silliness is an issue for many students, a class discussion can be an effective way to address the issue. Rather than doing all the talking, state the fact that too many silly antics will negatively affect students' learning and guide them in coming up with realistic solutions. Here are some tips for helping these discussions be productive:

- Tell children not to name others or describe an incident in a way that lets everyone know whom they're discussing.
- Hold these whole-class discussions only for issues that are continuous and involve many children. In response to a specific incident, address it privately with the children involved.
- Make sure all voices are heard and that children work together toward a solution.

Children often have a great deal of insight into what's causing the problem and what solutions might help. During one class discussion I held, my second graders let me know that after quiet time, they sometimes became silly because we went straight into math; they didn't feel they had a chance to reconnect after being on their own. We decided to play quick games or have brief partner chats to help with this transition.

Use problem-solving conferences

If the problem is with just one or two students, a problem-solving conference can offer similar benefits to them as a class discussion does for everyone. During these conferences, explore with a student why he's cracking jokes or being silly during serious lessons or discussions. Together, brainstorm strategies for the student to use to limit or prevent these instances from occurring.

To prepare for the conference, think about:

- ***What to say*** to begin the conference on a positive note.
- ***How to state the problem*** and its impact in concrete terms. For example: "Often you tell jokes during a serious classroom discussion or make funny faces to make the person next to you laugh."
- ***Possible causes of the problem.*** Be open to the child's ideas as to what's causing his behavior struggles. If the child is at a loss, name some possible reasons and see if he thinks any ring true.
- ***Strategies that may help,*** such as taking a break when he feels the impulse to make jokes or distract others, setting a designated time or two when he could tell a few jokes, or using a joke book in which he could record jokes or funny comments. Also encourage the child to offer strategies of his own, if any come to mind.

Consider an individual written agreement

Occasionally a student may develop a regular habit of fooling around or seeking attention at inappropriate times. For these situations, and after trying other strategies, you may want to use an individual written agreement to help the child gain control over when and how she uses humor at school.

It provides the child with a concrete goal to work toward, frequent feedback on how she's doing in meeting the goal, and, when appropriate, some extrinsic, nonmaterial reward.

Here's an example of one such an agreement:

- ***A clearly defined goal.*** "Lucia will stay focused during instructional time by looking at the speaker, listening, and refraining from making jokes."
- ***A reasonable standard for success*** in meeting the goal—"Lucia will be successful eighty percent of the time."
- ***A way to track success*** that's easy for the student to understand—check marks on a chart, for example.
- ***A nontangible reward*** for meeting the goal—"If successful, Lucia can spend time at the end of the day with a friend reading joke books."

Be empathetic

At times, you may notice a marked change in a child's behavior. Perhaps he's suddenly acting silly a lot more often. Such a change can be a sign of anxiety, stress, or another serious issue. Be understanding as you respond to the child. Try to find out what may be causing his change in behavior. Reach out to his parents, school counselors, and other school specialists.

Likewise, during stressful times at school or in the community, be prepared for some children to cope by acting extra silly or showing off more. Remind yourself to be patient, and seek support from colleagues as needed.

How to Talk With Parents About Silliness or Showing Off

As you think about how to approach parents about their child's difficulties with controlling silliness or sharing the spotlight, try to maintain a big picture perspective. During your teaching, children's jokes and laughter can derail learning and be frustrating. Yet in the grand scheme of things, too much silliness and showing off are usually just a temporary detour. Most children outgrow these behaviors (or channel them productively, as Jim Carrey did). You'll be more likely to maintain credibility and have parents hear you if you don't "oversell" silliness or showing off as a catastrophic problem.

When you discuss an incident with parents, describe the specific details of what's happening without ascribing negative intentions to their child's behavior or using charged words (even "silly" or "showing off" can have loaded connotations for parents). Also, let parents know why the behavior is a concern for the student's learning or relationships with classmates.

Remember to invite parents to share their observations. If a child is acting silly at school instead of focusing on a task, parents often see the same pattern at home. They may have strategies to suggest or offer other ways to help, and they may be more open to your suggestions if they have a chance to express their point of view.

Talking With Parents About Silliness or Showing Off	
Instead of labeling the behavior	**Describe the behavior, explain why it's a problem, and invite parent input**
"Justin is always trying to be the class clown. He can't stop showing off in front of his friends."	"Justin has a great sense of humor. But sometimes his jokes keep others from getting work done. We've been working together so he can figure out when to crack jokes and when to hold back. I'd like to share these ideas and hear your thoughts as well."
"Louise is such a giggle girl. The least little thing makes her laugh, and she's always trying to distract the people around her by making funny faces."	"Louise loves to laugh, but she sometimes struggles to regain her composure. Last week, we performed a poem and she couldn't stop laughing until she left the group. I'd like to share some strategies I'm using to help her maintain her composure and hear any ideas you have as well."
"Juan acts so young for his age. He's always fooling around when he's supposed to be working. He doesn't take anything seriously."	"At times, Juan gets carried away. Last week, he kept interrupting his friends' work and laughing. They didn't think it was funny and he didn't pick up on their cues. It's important for Juan to have fun in school, but he also needs to know when to stop. I want to share some strategies I'm teaching him. If you have strategies you use, I'd love to hear those, too."

At times, parents may turn to you for help with their child's silliness or showing off. If so, you may want to offer some of these suggestions:

- ***Help the child identify strengths*** other than joking. The positive feedback children often receive from joking (laughs from family and friends) can lead them to focus just on this area. Make sure children can shine in multiple ways.
- ***Be aware*** of how family members tend to use humor in various situations. Sometimes children model themselves after the adults in their lives.

- ***Discuss why seriousness matters*** at certain times. Do this at a neutral time, not when the child is "in trouble" for joking around—otherwise the topic will feel like a lecture.
- ***Respond to early signs*** that a child is beginning to act silly at inappropriate times. When adults respond early, it's easier for children to get back on track.

Closing Thoughts

All children need times to be silly and laugh. Some also thrive on opportunities to be the center of attention. But children also need plenty of focused time to learn and build academic and social skills. Balancing these needs can be challenging for us, but the work we do will pay off now and in the future for children. Students who learn how to switch from giggling to focus, to make appropriate choices about when to take center stage and when not to, and to productively channel their playfulness will be more likely to succeed in school.

Key Points

- Being silly and showing off are natural and healthy aspects of children's growth and development.
- Take proactive steps to balance fun and learning, such as by teaching children how to end the silliness and regain focus.
- Respond to silliness and showing off with empathy; remember, the quicker and "smaller" your response, the more effective it's likely to be.
- Avoid using labels such as "silly" or "showing off" when talking to parents about their child's behavior. Instead, describe the behavior objectively and ask parents for their thoughts.

8

Too Much Physical Contact

Too Much Physical Contact

Helping Children Learn Body Control

An energetic third grade student bounds over to the rug when the teacher signals it's time to begin the morning meeting. On his way there, he bumps into two classmates who call out with irritation, "Watch it, Michael!" He seems surprised—he barely noticed the contact. At the circle, Michael plops down and bumps into another student.

Later, at recess, he and a friend collide on the monkey bars as they cross in opposite directions. Soon they're playing a game in which they try to knock each other off the bars. Their behavior, although obviously playful, concerns the recess supervisor. He tells them to stop and they do. But when they start wrestling, the recess supervisor continues to keep an eye on them, not sure whether or how to intervene.

Like the recess supervisor, many teachers feel unsure about how to respond to these amiable but rough students. These children seem to have no ill intent. At the same time, they don't seem aware of the effect their bodies can have on others. They hug too hard, startle people by grabbing them, and wrestle, roughhouse, or race every chance they get.

While some classmates appreciate this physicality, many others do not. Those who have been at the receiving end of the roughhousing may be especially wary, on guard, and distracted from learning. As classmates start to give them a wide berth, children who are too rough also lose out academically and socially.

In this chapter, you'll learn why students are overly physical, how to teach them to be more aware of their bodies, ways to respond when they're too rough, and tips for talking with parents about a child's excessive physicality.

Why Children Get Too Physical

Often, children who get overly physical are simply trying to meet their physical needs. Picture two boys wrestling as the class transitions from one academic task to another. Most likely, they've been sitting too long. All their pent-up energy needs an outlet—they simply need the release this rough play provides. And some children—boys *and* girls—have stronger needs for movement and activity than others. As a result, they'll look for ways to meet those needs throughout the school day.

To meet their physical needs

When you think about children who are frequently restless or too physical, keep in mind that all children need opportunities every day for play and physical activity. It wasn't that long ago when many school-age children walked or biked to school, had two long recesses a day, and played outside after school, on weekends, and throughout the summer. Our schools and society may have become more sedentary, but children's need for physical activity has not changed.

To feel a sense of belonging and significance

Children who are too physical are sometimes just trying to meet their need to connect with others. Lacking other ways to get noticed or engage classmates, these children instead wrestle them or show their interest in other physical ways. It may also be that their family members use physical gestures—a slap on the back or a playful body bump—to show affection.

If Touching Has Sexual Overtones or Is Done in Anger

The goal of this book is to address common behavior challenges, so extreme issues of physicality are beyond its scope. Examples of this include:

- reacting violently, such as hitting classmates or teachers after a perceived insult
- touching that appears sexual in nature, which may be a sign of abuse

If you observe or learn about an incident such as these, follow school and district guidelines for reporting and addressing it.

Lack of body control skills

Some students have not yet fully developed the ability to manage their body movements in appropriate ways for a given situation. They may also not know how to switch from vigorous physical play to a lower "volume" when necessary.

Lack of social skills

Some children may also be unaware that their classmates find rough contact unwelcome. When they bump into classmates or hug them too hard, they simply don't pick up on nonverbal cues that indicate displeasure or unease.

Physicality and child development

Many children, especially boys, need a great deal of physical movement throughout childhood. But the physical changes children experience at certain ages can exacerbate existing tendencies to be overly physical, to wrestle, or to roughhouse. If you teach at the grade levels in the following chart, be prepared to find many productive outlets for this energy and help children understand what sorts of physical contact are socially acceptable at school.

Some Child Development Characteristics Related to Physicality		
Grade	Characteristic	Influence on Being Overly Physical
Kindergarten (ages 4–6)	• Need lots of physical activity • Often fall out of chairs	• May not be used to the sitting and inactivity school requires • Need more intense and more frequent physical breaks • Have not yet developed much body control
3rd (ages 7–9)	• Very energetic and active • Often experiencing a growth spurt • May feel restless and need to move a great deal	• May need more chances to move and be physical than school provides • Feel awkward, uncomfortable, and less in control during and shortly after growth spurt
4th (ages 8–10)	• Can feel restless physically • Often like to roughhouse and wrestle	• Need many opportunities to move and have physical contact and may not get enough of these at school • Use roughhousing or wrestling to make and keep friends

By understanding children's needs for play and physical activity, we can better empathize with their struggles to sit still and stay on task—at any age or grade—and help them meet their needs in productive, healthy ways.

Keeping Body Movements in Control

Proactive Steps to Take

A few simple actions can go a long way toward helping students who need a lot of physical activity succeed academically and socially. It's especially important to help them find appropriate physical outlets and teach them limits for movement and contact in school spaces.

Discuss how classroom rules govern physical actions

As teachers, we need to have a clear idea of the line between acceptable and unacceptable physical contact—and teach that distinction to children. For instance, if you decide that friendly jostling is OK, but full-out wrestling is not, teach students that expectation rather than assuming they'll know.

You might start this discussion by saying, "Our rules say that we will be kind to each other. Sometimes, we show kindness by being physical with our friends—for instance, by giving a hug or a high five. How can we be kind to each other and still take care of each other's bodies?" Creating a chart with students like the one shown, using students' own words as much as possible, can be especially helpful to this teaching.

Taking Care of Each Other and Our Bodies

	Looks like	Sounds like	Feels like
In the classroom	• Watching out for other people • Staying in your rug space or at your desk • Gentle high fives, hugs, fist bumps, chest bumps	• Apologizing if you bump into someone • Stopping if someone asks you to stop • Using kind words with any bumps, high fives, etc.	• Friendly • Happy • Gentle • Safe
At recess	• Using monkey bars or the slide one person at a time • Watching where you run • Avoiding rough play during soccer, basketball, etc.	• Loud but friendly sounds • "Watch out, here I come!" • Apologizing if you smack into a person	• Friendly • Competitive but not in a mean way • Happy • Safe for all

Also, try to remind students of the class rules before a potentially tricky situation, such as having to sit still during a closing circle sharing at the end of the day.

Provide plenty of physical outlets

Because so much wrestling and roughhousing results from pent-up energy, the best antidote is to give students chances throughout the day to release that energy in positive ways. Here are a few ideas:

- ***Have recess every day, if possible.*** Make sure students have a chance to enjoy a physically active daily recess. If some students need more physical activity, consider extending recess if possible, scheduling a second, briefer recess, or taking the class for a quick walk around the building.
- ***Include games and energizers.*** Plan short activities and movement breaks (one to three minutes each) throughout the day. Make sure at least some involve gross motor movements, and model and teach what these movements should look and feel like. For resources on fun games and energizers, see page 258.
- ***Energize academic tasks.*** When possible, provide opportunities for students to act out stories, stand up during partner chats, or do jumping jacks or chant as they practice math facts. Try to choose themes that lend themselves to physical activity, such as action stories and dramatic historical events.
- ***Individualize.*** Some students may need even more physical activity. When you see signs of restlessness, send the student on an errand, invite her to do push-ups against the wall, or even allow her to take a supervised walk around the building.

Teach impulse control

Teach what it looks like to resist an impulse, and give students plenty of practice in exercising this self-control. For instance, use Interactive Modeling with a think-aloud to show having an impulse to reach over and nudge a friend and then deciding to rub your hands vigorously together instead. Make practicing impulse control fun by playing games requiring fast starting and stopping—try a freeze dance or Simon Says.

Promote perspective-taking

Students who are too rough often don't understand how their actions affect others. They may not yet be able to grasp that others see things differently from the way they do. Have conversations in class about the different ways people might respond to overly vigorous gestures and play. These types of discussions help children hear what others have to say and get a chance to explain themselves as well.

Reevaluate classroom space

Sometimes jostling and horseplay ensue when students sit too close together or don't have room to move freely. In a crowded space, a bump can quickly escalate into roughhousing. Try to arrange the instructional space, circle area, and children's desks so that all students have sufficient personal space.

Although increasing class sizes make this a challenge for many of us, think creatively about the space you have. For example, can the table where you meet with small groups also serve as the art or science area? See pages 256 and 258 for resources on making the best use of classroom space.

Reinforce students' efforts at body control

Students who struggle to manage their physical energy need encouragement, so look for small moments of self-control that you can reinforce (in private). This helps children recognize their progress and gives them something positive to build on for the future. See the table on the next page for some examples of reinforcing language.

Reinforcing Language in Action

If a situation like this happens	Try this
A student who often gets too boisterous during and after a movement break stays in control and focuses back on the lesson as soon as it restarts.	"Allen, you stayed in your own personal space and had fun without bumping into anyone. You're learning self-control!"
Two students often greet each other with slamming chest bumps or wild wrestling moves. Today, they settle for a calm high five.	"That is just how we practiced—a fun, friendly greeting that's gentle enough for our classroom!"
A student often has trouble staying in her personal space, frequently sprawling into others' areas. Today, she remains in her seat and writes.	"Lauren, you stayed in your personal space for all of writing time. What helped you do that today?"

If a child is overly sensitive to other children's physicality . . .

Sometimes children overreact to any physical contact. After a small accidental bump in line, for example, a child may complain, "Jason smacked into me!" If you have a child who takes offense at the slightest touch, help him recognize that some physical contact is unavoidable and appropriate in a group setting.

Guide him in sorting out examples of incidental touching from actual rough contact, and reinforce his progress at making that distinction. Reinforce his progress when he bounces back despite having some small contact with a classmate. Before situations that might involve some jostling, such as transitions, remind the student of that possibility. For more strategies on building coping skills, see pages 234–238.

Stopping the Rough Stuff

How to Respond Effectively in the Moment

Despite all our proactive teaching, children may still act too roughly. Keep in mind that most of these children aren't deliberately trying to disrupt our lessons or cause harm to others. Nevertheless, the main goal of our response is the same as for most other misbehaviors: stop the problem behavior and get the lesson back on track as quickly as possible. Here are some tips.

Respond early

The sooner you respond when children are becoming too physical, the easier it will be for them to regain control of their bodies. When a child has just begun tapping a neighbor, it takes much less effort for her to stop and put her hands down than if her tapping has already turned into roughhousing.

Use clear redirecting language

Students who are being too rough generally respond best to a clear, public redirection. (Responding publicly lets all the other children know that this behavior is unacceptable.) In a matter-of-fact tone, tell them exactly what to do, especially with the body parts that are getting them into trouble.

When responding, resist having the student immediately reflect on how others might feel. In the heat of the moment, they can't access the logical parts of their mind. Allow some time to pass before asking them to reflect on their behavior.

TEACHING TIP

Watch for Power Differences

Some children may use their physical advantages to intimidate others. Even a seemingly minor act, such as tripping or jostling in line, could be a sign of bullying behavior, especially if one child is bigger or stronger than the other.

If you think that power differences exist, take immediate action to stop the behavior. To learn more, read *How to Bullyproof Your Classroom* by Caltha Crowe (Northeast Foundation for Children, 2012) and search "bullyproofing" at www.responsiveclassroom.org.

Redirecting Language in Action

If a situation like this happens	Try this
A child who struggles with personal boundaries hugs a classmate, who looks uncomfortable.	"Janelle, move back to your space and put your hands in your lap."
A student who gets very animated during discussions grabs a classmate's shoulders and shakes her slightly as he makes his point.	"Elliott, take your hands off Maria. Now, try to convince her of your point with your hands touching only the air."
While you are discussing something with a colleague, you see two boys who often wrestle begin to poke each other.	"Armand, Alec, move apart." (Pause to watch to make sure they do.)

Use appropriate logical consequences

Sometimes, the most effective way to help students who are having difficulty keeping their hands and bodies off others is to use a well-chosen logical consequence. Such consequences can remove them from a tempting situation and give them a chance to bring their energy level back down. As always, use a respectful tone and save the discussion about the incident for later.

When using time-out for these students, consider modifying it so that it involves doing something physical in the time-out spot—for example, push-ups against the wall or squats behind a chair. Requiring students who have lots of energy to sit still in one spot may set them up for failure.

Logical Consequences in Action

If a situation like this happens	Try this
During writing time, a child who struggles with personal boundaries leans over and rests her head on a classmate's arm. The classmate asks her to move and she does, but she soon resumes leaning against her classmate.	**Loss of privilege:** "Janelle, you need to work in our private area for now." **Follow up later:** "What was going on for you? Why might that behavior be a problem for Dawn? What will help you follow the rules next time?"
A student who gets very animated while working knocks over another student's project.	**You break it, you fix it:** "Elliott, see if Reyna wants your help getting her display back in order."
The principal comes to the door to discuss an administrative issue. When you turn back to your class, you see that two boys are fully engaged in wrestling.	**Time-out:** "Armand, Alec. Both of you take a break." **Follow up later:** "Why do you think I sent you to time-out? Why might that behavior be a problem for our class? What will help you follow the rules next time?"

Ask colleagues for help

Ordinarily, most children regain self-control with a redirection or logical consequence, but some may have trouble stopping even in the time-out spot or go right back to the problematic behavior immediately after the time-out. In these situations, try using the buddy teacher procedure that was explained on pages 34–35.

If a Child Continues to Struggle

Despite all our efforts, some children may continue to have difficulties managing their bodies. If so, continue using the proactive strategies on pages 194–198, and responding effectively in the moment. In addition, try these next steps.

Establish a private signal

Teach the child a signal to use when she needs a physical break. After giving the signal, she could engage in a previously agreed upon activity, such as jumping jacks in the hall or a short walk.

Invite the student to strategize with you

Some students need more individual support to learn how to recognize the impact of their actions. Use a problem-solving conference to talk with a student about why being too physical is problematic for him and others. To prepare for the conference, think about:

- ***What to say*** to begin the conference on a positive note.
- ***How to state the problem*** and its impact in concrete terms. For example: "I've noticed that you sometimes bump into other people and wrestle with John. That distracts your classmates and can be dangerous."
- ***Possible causes of the problem.*** If the child can't explain what's causing his rough behavior, state some possible reasons and see if he thinks any ring true. Or, you might ask questions, such as "Could it be that you want to be friends with John and you're using wrestling to show him that?"
- ***Strategies that may help,*** such as a private signal, "I need a break" cards the child could use to show when he needs a physical outlet, or special time with certain friends (if you suspect he's being too physical out of a need for belonging). Also encourage the child to think of some strategies of his own to offer.

Help the child find other outlets

When it seems that a child might benefit from additional physical activity, you may want to encourage the child's parents to sign her up for an after-school sports program or activity club. Some parents may not realize the benefits of such programs or the financial help that's available. If the parents are unable to accommodate an extracurricular activity, work with coaches and PE teachers to find additional channels for the child's energy during the school day.

Consider an individual written agreement

Some students may continue to be too physical even after you've tried several different strategies. For these children, an individual written agreement might give them the impetus they need to learn when and how to control their bodies. This agreement provides the child with a concrete goal to work toward, frequent feedback on how he's doing in meeting the goal, and, when appropriate, some extrinsic, nonmaterial reward. Here's an example of one such an agreement:

- ***A clearly defined goal.*** "William will keep hands, feet, and body to himself."
- ***A reasonable standard for success*** in meeting the goal—"William will be successful seventy-five percent of the time."
- ***A way to track success*** that's simple for the student to understand—craft sticks in a jar, for example.
- ***A nontangible reward*** for meeting the goal—"If successful, William can help Coach Rhonda set up for PE."

How to Talk With Parents About Excessive Physicality

Once, when I was getting ready to have a parent-teacher conference about a child who was overly physical, I was met with a hearty slap on the back from the child's dad. After regaining my balance, I mentally stopped to appreciate this reminder—children learn from their families. Keep this idea in mind when you talk with parents about a child who's being too rough with classmates.

Also, know that some parents may rush to their child's defense by asserting that "He never means any harm" or "She just has lots of energy." Help these parents recognize that even well-meaning behavior can have negative consequences. Acknowledge the lack of malicious intent and then explain why the behavior is problematic to the child and her classmates.

It's also important not to push parents' red alert button. Avoid placing labels on the child or his behavior. Instead, describe what you see and are doing in a matter-of-fact way.

At times, parents may turn to you for help when their child is too boisterous or rough at home. If that happens, you may want to offer some of these suggestions:

- ***Make sure the child has outlets*** for his physical energy. Try to give him multiple chances to be outdoors and actively play with others, or encourage him to join a sports team or club.
- ***Model appropriate body control.*** Sometimes adults unintentionally exhibit the very behaviors we find problematic in children. Be aware of modeling roughhousing.
- ***Respond quickly and calmly*** to early signs that the child is having difficulty controlling his body or energy level. This will help keep the child from harm, as well as give him a chance to meet his needs in more acceptable way.

Closing Thoughts

As teachers, we move throughout the day, so it's easy to get annoyed by children's constant wriggling, pushing, and jostling—and forget that they need to move, too. By providing meaningful outlets for play and physical activity throughout the school day, we can help promote their well-being. Our goal should not be to stamp out children's physical energy, but to channel it productively and help them learn how to manage it on their own.

Key Points

- Children need to play and be physically active every day.

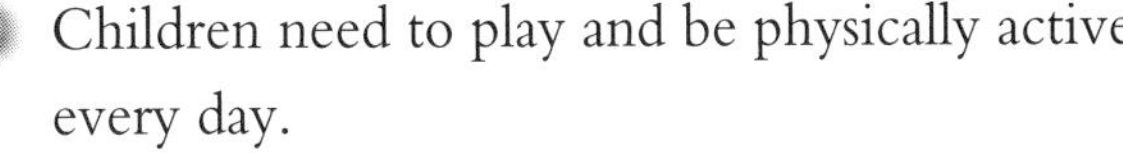

- Provide children with enriching ways to use their physical energy, such as by using energizers and other movement breaks and by including physical activity in lessons when possible.
- Respond to children who are being too rough with a quick redirection or an appropriate logical consequence, such as a time-out with a physical component.
- Work with parents to find ways to help their child use their physical energy in productive, healthy ways.

9

Dishonesty

Dishonesty

Setting Children Up for Success With Honesty

The range of behaviors related to dishonesty in school is wide and varied—fibbing (telling lies), cheating, blaming others, and making unfounded excuses are just a few examples. When I think about these issues and the students I taught, I often return to one memorable experience. At first glance, this student's actions may appear extreme, but it's fairly typical of the challenges students face with honesty.

As a teacher, I kept a daily conversation journal with each student. They'd write me a note each morning; I'd write back that night. One year, a student named Callie and I began by corresponding about a bike accident she had

been in that summer. In excruciating detail, Callie described the crash, her mother's panicked reaction, and the wounds she suffered. Because it usually took a while to get into a groove with these journals, I remember being excited that the writing relationship between us was off to such a good start.

Then, I discovered one small problem—none of what Callie had written was true. When she took her journal home, her mom read it, and showed up with Callie the next morning to tell me that it was all fiction—there had been no accident. I was taken aback, but I was also very curious.

I asked Callie what the whole thing had been about. She shrugged, as children do, but then she said, "I wanted to have something interesting to talk about. Nothing interesting happens to me." Now I saw that, however unintentionally, these journals might make some students feel pressure to embellish or invent things to make themselves appear more interesting. Nonetheless, I calmly told her that while she could write fictional stories in her other journals, in this one, the expectation was to tell true stories.

Callie's experience isn't uncommon for young children as they begin to explore the world and their place in it. What began as a lie to impress me grew until she couldn't see a way out of it.

My experience with Callie led me to reflect on how important it is that we adults respond with empathy and clarity when children make mistakes with truth-telling—rather than labeling or punishing them. Punitive responses can lead to more dishonesty, as children will go to great lengths to keep us from finding things out, out of fear of our judgment or punishment.

This chapter focuses on four common misbehaviors related to dishonesty in school, but much of the information can be adapted for other forms of dishonesty. The following four misbehaviors probably won't surprise you, but they can be tricky to deal with—and cause great harm to the classroom community and children's learning:

- cheating on a test or quiz
- telling a lie (or making up or embellishing a story)
- denying responsibility for something said or done
- taking something impulsively

In this chapter, we'll explore why children behave in less-than-honest ways, how to support children to be truthful and honest, how to respond effectively if a child makes a mistake and behaves dishonestly, and strategies for discussing these behaviors with parents.

Why Do Children Sometimes Fail at Honesty?

Children tell fibs, cheat, and take things for many reasons, including to meet their needs for belonging and significance. Developmental factors often influence honesty, as children have to learn the difference between what's true and what's not, when a "white lie" might be kinder than the cold truth, and other sticky honesty issues.

Some children may act dishonestly at times because they lack certain social skills, particularly impulse control. They havn't yet learned when to give in to impulses and when to resist them. They may also not know how to rein in their impulses even when they know it's wrong to act on them. Here are some common reasons why children behave in dishonest ways.

To protect themselves

The human need for self-preservation can lead children to act dishonestly. For instance, if children know that the adults in their lives will punish them whenever they do something wrong, they're more likely to deny a misdeed in order to stay out of trouble. Similarly, children who've been penalized or shamed over their academic performance may take shortcuts, such as copying others' work, to get better results and avoid these punishments.

To feel significant

Children sometimes exaggerate, embellish, or even make up stories about their lives because they want to stand out to their classmates and teachers. They may feel as if their experiences are not as worthwhile or exciting as their classmates'.

Trying to feel significant is often a factor when children make excuses or deny wrongdoing. A child may worry that if she admits doing something wrong, then her teacher or classmates will think less of her. To avoid these results and maintain her sense of importance, she stretches the truth.

Similarly, stealing something may give some children a sense of power. They may like the excitement of secretly taking things or possessing a forbidden object. They may even feel that these actions prove that they have a special talent. Other children may take things to seek revenge for when their feelings were hurt and their sense of significance was diminished.

To feel a sense of belonging

Children also may tell a lie to feel more connected to others. Because they want classmates to believe that they have something in common, children may lie about their interests or experiences. "I play on a soccer team, too," one child might say to another student known for his love of the game.

In older elementary grades, stealing may serve a similar purpose. The more students' status is determined by what they own—cool clothes, the latest techno-gadget—the more likely they'll be tempted to take these objects.

Lack of impulse control

Sometimes children act dishonestly because they lack the skill of impulse control. Seeing something interesting, a child grabs it. Or a child notices that a classmate has a different answer and copies it because it seems better.

Children in these situations may also feel trapped afterward. Returning an impulsively grabbed object or admitting cheating may subject the child to judgment by the teacher and classmates. Many children (and adults) don't know how to dig themselves out of the trouble their impulsivity has caused. They're unsure how to face up to what they've done and lack the skills to make amends.

Honesty and child development

Developmental factors also influence a child's ability to be honest. For instance, young children may tell a tall tale because they're still figuring out the difference between fact and fiction. Likewise, they may take something that belongs to another child because they haven't figured out the rules for property ownership. They may cheat on a test because they don't see copying someone's answers as akin to stealing someone's belongings. As with many behaviors, children of all ages often need to experiment to find out what's acceptable and what's not in various situations.

Some Child Development Characteristics Related to Struggles With Honesty

Grade	Characteristic	Influence on honesty
Kindergarten (ages 4–6)	• Value adult approval • Think out loud • Still figuring out difference between reality and fantasy	• Not yet sure what's true and what's not • May tell a lie to avoid getting in trouble • May speak impulsively
3rd (ages 7–9)	• Very social • Tend to exaggerate	• May be dishonest in ways that promote their social status (bragging about things they don't have, taking a popular object, etc.) • May stretch the truth to impress others
6th (ages 10–12)	• Very social • Worry about who's "in" and who's "out"	• May lie to impress others or put others down • May take objects that would increase social appeal • May cheat at schoolwork or games to appear more capable and successful

If you teach at these grade levels, be especially thoughtful about teaching why telling the truth and respecting property are important and how dishonesty can negatively affect students' learning and relationships.

Understanding the needs children are trying to address through dishonest behaviors does not mean that we condone their missteps. But we also don't need to overreact to those behaviors. Instead, it's helpful to view children's missteps as teaching opportunities for us and learning opportunities for them.

Being Truthful and Respecting Others' Things

Proactive Steps to Promote Honesty

Children need to learn why being honest and trustworthy matters. When they feel cared for in a supportive learning environment, they're better able to develop this understanding along with skills related to honesty. The more time you devote to creating a positive community, to communicating your expectations about honesty (and the reasons behind them), and to building up students' social skills, the more honest your students will be.

Foster positive relationships with students

It's much harder to lie to or take something from a person who cares about you, or cheat in the classroom of a teacher whom you respect. Get to know your students and help each one feel cared for in your classroom. For example, try to connect with each student—at arrival, lunch, or other less structured times. You may even want to take notes on what you know about each child and how often you've communicated with him (see page 97 for tips).

When a student has been untruthful or taken something from you, a healthy student-teacher bond will also help her accept responsibility. To preserve these relationships, be mindful when children make mistakes. Deal with the issue respectfully—and then move on. This way, children will know that you're not judging them or holding anything against them.

Promote student relationships

When students feel connected to their classmates, they're less likely to act dishonestly to impress others or feel powerful. They're also more likely to admit to mistakes because they'll be less worried about classmates being unkind to them when they do. Devote time to community-building and "getting to know you" activities at the start of school and throughout the year. Frequently mix up pairs and groups so that children have a chance to interact with all their classmates.

Normalize mistake-making

Teach students that mistakes are part of learning and life. When children feel that they can make mistakes without invoking the wrath of others, they may not feel the need to lie to cover up a mistake. Similarly, when students understand that learning, not perfection, is the goal, they're less likely to cheat on tests or assignments.

To foster an appreciation of mistakes and help children learn to accept responsibility for them, have students write and share about mistakes they've made. Reading children's books together can also provide great starting points for discussing mistakes. (For a list of helpful children's books, see pages 252–255.)

Connect classroom rules to honesty and trustworthiness

Class rules should address being honest and respecting others' property. As you discuss rules such as "take care of each other" and "be responsible," call students' attention to what these mean in terms of telling the truth, doing one's own work, and admitting to mistakes. Together, flesh out how telling the truth might look, sound, and feel in a variety of situations. For instance, create a chart like the one on the next page.

What Telling the Truth Looks, Sounds, and Feels Like When Playing a Competitive Game		
Looks like	**Sounds like**	**Feels like**
• Admit when someone tags you, scored a goal, etc. • Admit when you're out, have to miss a turn, etc. • Follow the rules even if it means you lose.	• "I'm out." • "It's your point." • "You tagged me." • "I have to miss my turn."	• Fair • Proud • Difficult to do, but rewarding

Acknowledge the challenge of being honest

Telling the truth is not as straightforward as it sounds. By the time they enter school, children have usually heard adults stretch the truth. For example, we might tell someone on the phone, "I can't talk right now," and then sit down to read a magazine. We may tell a friend, "Your dress looks great!" only to say to someone else later, "What was she thinking?"

Explore issues of honesty with empathy while still holding high expectations. Before a game, you might say, "We're about to play a partner game in math. I know how much everyone loves to win these games and it can be tempting to bend the rules. Why is it important to follow these rules?" Or, when teaching children how to take responsibility for a mistake, you might say, "It takes courage to tell the truth because we aren't sure how the other person is going to react."

It's also helpful to share a time when you struggled with honesty. For instance: "Last night a friend asked me to help her with a project. I was tempted to make up some excuse. Instead, I was honest and said, 'I'd love to another time, but I was planning to finish my book.'" Sharing these experiences with students also shows you trust them, fostering their sense of significance.

Teach children what taking responsibility looks and sounds like

Children's dishonesty often occurs when they make excuses for or deny making a mistake. Sometimes they do this because they don't know what it looks and sounds like to take responsibility for their actions. You can use Interactive Modeling or role-play to give children meaningful practice with these very challenging skills.

Use role-play if you want students to brainstorm many possible ways to own up to mistakes in sticky situations, such as spilling paint on someone else's art project. When you want to teach and practice one specific way, use Interactive Modeling. For example, use Interactive Modeling to show what it looks and sounds like to say, "That was my mistake. I'm sorry." For more on role-play and Interactive Modeling, see pages 24–25.

Be a model of honesty for students

Small unkept promises—"We'll have five extra minutes of recess another day to make up for today"—can confuse students. Worse, it might lead them to believe that you say you value honesty, but don't live out that belief. Be as truthful and as forthright as you can be about any mistakes you make.

Set students up for success with sharing and writing

Giving students time to share what's happening in their lives is a powerful way to build significance and community. However, be careful to set up these opportunities so that students don't feel a need to make things up or exaggerate.

- ***Welcome a variety of everyday topics.*** After my experience with Callie (page 207), I made sure to model writing about everyday events whenever I introduced conversation journals. Provide students with topics or brainstorm ones that everyone can feel comfortable sharing about orally or in writing. For instance, model sharing or writing about a pet, favorite food, or family tradition. Avoid assigning topics such as vacation trips or special toys, as these might prompt some children to stretch the truth.

- ***Monitor for competitiveness.*** If you get the sense that sharing or writing time has become too competitive, with students vying to outdo one another with stories of exotic trips or new acquisitions, take the reins back. Remodel and assign more neutral topics for a week or two (for example, a person students admire and why, or a book they love and why). Or go in the other direction and make it "tall tale" week or assign an imaginative topic (for example, a new invention for the future).

- ***Teach how to respond respectfully.*** Model and practice with students how to make respectful comments and ask appropriate questions based on what their classmates share. Knowing that their classmates will respond with care encourages children to share about actual events and what's really important to them.

TEACHING TIP

Limit What Students Bring to School

Toys or electronics brought from home can alter the social dynamics of the classroom, creating a climate in which children feel defined by what they have or don't have. As a result, students may find it harder to resist the temptation to take someone else's prized possession.

To help prevent such a climate from developing, set a clear policy about what students can bring to school—inform parents of it—and hold students to the policy.

Teach caring for supplies

A child may also justify taking things if the owner doesn't seem to value them in the first place. She may think, "No one cares about this. It was crammed back here in the cabinet." Take the time to keep materials organized and in good working condition, and show students how to care for them. Also teach children to care for their own belongings the same way (for example, by keeping loose items in zipped-up backpacks).

Reinforce children's efforts at honesty

Be sure to recognize children's attempts to speak and act honestly, especially if this is an area in which they struggle. When children admit that they've done something wrong, avoid immediately focusing on their mistake. Instead, acknowledge students in private for their honesty.

Reinforcing Language in Action	
If a situation like this happens	**Try this (in private)**
Claire often tells exaggerated stories at sharing time. This morning, she shares a straightforward story about going to the movies with a friend and seeing a classmate there.	"Claire, your sharing let us learn more about what you enjoy doing. Did you see how interested everyone was? Did you notice Jen's excitement when you said that you saw her?"
A child's special pen is missing. Lara brings it to you at the end of the day, saying, "I'm sorry. I took this. I know I shouldn't have."	"I know it can be hard to admit when you made a mistake. That took real courage. What do you want to do next?"
Liam rarely takes responsibility for mistakes. Today he's playing a math game with a classmate who says, "Liam, you only get one card." Liam puts the extra card back and says, "I'm sorry. You're right."	"Liam, in the card game, I noticed that you quickly put the card back and kept going. You're learning to take responsibility for your mistakes. How did that feel?"

If a Child Behaves Dishonestly

How to Respond Effectively in the Moment

Once a child has said something that isn't true or taken an item that doesn't belong to him, how we respond is critical. We cannot undo these acts, but we can make matters worse. Our first instinct may be to scold the child, but this can be humiliating to him—and make it more likely that he'll repeat the behavior.

Instead, address the issue with empathy and in private. Ideally, our careful response will help prevent future incidents, teach the value of honesty, and restore a sense of community.

Don't take it personally

It can hurt when a student looks you in the eye and fibs, or you discover that a student has cheated on an assignment. It may feel even worse if a student takes something from you or a classmate. While it's natural to feel affronted, try to let it go. Remember that the child's actions have more to do with her needs or development and little, if anything, to do with you. If you feel upset, wait until you're calm to address the issue.

Think about the child's underlying motivation

The words "lie," "cheat," and "steal" do not perfectly fit every situation. In the classroom, thinking of every untruth as a lie can lead to problems. If a child tells the class he has a pet when in fact he does not, is it really a lie? Or is he expressing a wish? If, after a school break, a student makes up an exotic vacation tale because she knows some of her classmates have gone on actual vacations, does the word "lie" really apply? Before responding to a child's statement, think carefully about what may be going on with her.

Address the issue privately

When a child makes a mistake regarding honesty, it's tempting to call her on it publicly. However, publicly addressing dishonesty may embarrass her and diminish her sense of self-worth. Instead, try to address the issue while saving the child from embarrassment.

For instance, if a child launches into a story at sharing time that you know is false, you might say, "Marta, I'm sorry to interrupt, but I want to touch base with you about this topic. You can share later." If you don't feel comfortable responding in the moment, let the child continue, but talk to her later in private. Point out what you know, ask questions, and explain why her dishonesty was problematic. For example:

> "Marta, I want to talk about what you shared this morning. Your story about going to Antarctica was entertaining—maybe you could write about it. I want to remind you that our morning meeting is a time to share true stories. When you tell made-up stories then, it might make people doubt other things you share. I'll help you write great stories and also learn how to share about your real life."

If you're worried that other students may think that your failure to act in the moment is an endorsement of the mistake, address the issue in public as minimally as possible. For example: "Marta, let's talk later about your story."

Give children an "out"

If a child has told a lie or taken something impulsively—and then doesn't know how to get out of the situation—look for a simple solution. For instance, if something in the classroom has been taken, you might say, "Kim's new sunglasses are missing. If you happen to find them, put them on my desk. She needs to have them back by the time we go home."

Use logical consequences wisely

- ***If a child has taken something or told a lie.*** When you see or learn that a child has taken something, the most logical consequence to use is making reparations. For instance, he returns the item, or replaces it if it's lost for good or damaged.

  If a child tells a lie and it has a direct effect on another student, you can use a similar consequence to guide the child to make amends. For example, he can simply correct the initial statement. An apology or other reparation is also appropriate—as long as the apology is not forced. Again, try to keep conversations about these incidents private, limited to the students involved in the situation.

Logical Consequences in Action: Reparations ("you break it, you fix it")

If a situation like this happens	Try this
Andre tells an untrue story about his friend Trey to two of their classmates. Trey hears about it.	"Andre, you need to let Sam and Martin know that what you said about Trey was not true. How else can you help Trey feel better?"
During a math quiz, Liza copies from the paper of the child next to her.	"Liza, you'll need to make up this quiz. I'll devise a different one. You can either take it at choice time today or arrival time tomorrow."
Mandy secretly takes a CD from the music room. She puts it in her backpack and it breaks. She tells a classmate, who reports it to you.	"Mandy, once we figure out how much it will cost to replace the CD, we'll make a plan for how you'll pay for it." (For example, she could bring in her money from home or help with certain tasks in the music room.)

➤ ***If a child denies responsibility.*** When you see a child break a rule, you may want to use a logical consequence even if he denies the behavior. Calmly give the consequence. Then, if the child accepts it, consider the problem addressed—and move on. Take the acceptance of the consequence as his admission and resist getting into a power struggle. No one wins if you try to force the child to say, "I did it."

Logical Consequences in Action: When a Child Denies Responsibility

If a situation like this happens	Try this
You see a child who keeps rolling her eyes at her friends while another classmate tells about her weekend.	**Use time-out:** Teacher: "Lila, take a break." Lila: "I didn't do anything." Teacher: "Take a break. We can talk later."

CONTINUED ON PAGE 221

If a situation like this happens	Try this
Your colleague tells you that two students are making a lot of noise in the boys' bathroom. You knock on the door, open it, and see paper towels, toilet paper, and water everywhere. The students claim, "We didn't do it. It was like this when we came in."	**Use reparation:** "The bathroom needs to be cleaned. I'll watch you get started." They immediately start cleaning. Stay for a minute and then say something like, "You're off to a great start. It looks like this should take about three more minutes. I'll come back then."
You send Erika on an errand. An office administrator brings her back a few minutes later and tells you that Erika was running and yelling, "Hello!" at every room she passed. Erika quickly says, "I didn't mean to do that!"	**Use time-out, then loss of privilege:** Now: "Erika, take a break so that you'll be ready to rejoin us for reading." Later: "Erika, for the next two days, an adult will walk with you in the halls. I know you'll be able to walk quietly on your own after that."

This advice assumes that you've taught and prepared students for the use of logical consequences. Specifically, children need to be ready for the possibility that you may send them to time-out or give them another consequence even if they don't know why or disagree. In these situations, teach them to go to the time-out space without arguing, and then discuss the issue with you later. For more on using logical consequences, see pages 32–34.

➤ ***If you're not sure, refrain from imposing consequences.*** When you have a strong feeling that a child was responsible for a problem, but are not 100 percent sure, try to let the incident go. These circumstances are often hard to accept, but the reality is that you can't force a child to admit to wrongdoing—and you can't in good conscience impose a consequence when you're not sure yourself. Whenever you're not sure, refrain even from making insinuations that you believe the child is at fault.

Reacting respectfully, but matter-of-factly, when children make mistakes with honesty will send them a powerful message about the expectations and value of truthfulness. But our reactions are just part of the information children need to learn; remember to keep coming back to the proactive strategies on pages 212–217 as well.

If a Child Continues to Struggle

Some children, despite all your efforts, may still have a hard time telling the truth or leaving tempting items alone. They may have deeper issues with feeling significant, or they may have developed habits they need help in breaking. With these children, try some of the following ideas.

Teach the use of a private signal

For children who struggle with telling the truth, teach them that when you give a signal, such as a tug on the ear, they should stop talking. Use this signal when a child starts telling a story that clearly isn't true or begins to get herself into another tricky situation.

Hold a problem-solving conference

A problem-solving conference can help a child develop strategies to use before he finds himself in situations where he's tempted to tell lies, cheat, or take something impulsively. It can also help him learn how to stop himself when he's already in those situations. Prepare for the conference by thinking through the following:

- ***What you will say*** to get the conference started on a positive note.
- ***How you will present the problem*** and its effects. For example, "I've noticed that sometimes you say things that aren't true. Last week, you said you had finished your project, but you hadn't. You told Ted that you were on a basketball team, but your mom said that's not true. If you say things that aren't true, people may stop trusting you."
- ***What you'll propose as possible reasons*** for the behavior and how you'll invite the child's input as well.
- ***Possible solutions you'll propose.*** For example, the student might have a special signal he can give when he's said something untrue so you can help him in the moment; he might go to a cool-down spot when tempted to lie; or he could keep a notebook of falsehoods he was tempted to say but didn't.

Help the child find productive ways to feel significant

Children who repeatedly behave dishonestly may feel isolated from their classmates. In addition to the previous strategies, think of ways to help these children recognize their talents and skills and help their classmates see these qualities as well.

For some children, you may want to start with storytelling or writing. This allows them to channel their imaginations in productive ways and bolsters their academic skills. Even if you're doing a fact-based unit, you might modify a child's assignments to allow for fiction or exaggeration. You may also want to more intentionally help the child develop and maintain stronger friendships with classmates, and spend more time with the child yourself.

Seek help from colleagues if needed

In some situations, a child may have strongly established habits of fibbing, cheating, or taking things. Even with all your work, and the help of parents, the child may not make as much progress as you'd expect. If so, talk with a school counselor, an administrator, or a trusted colleague about other steps to try.

How to Talk With Parents About Struggles With Honesty

Because honesty issues have moral overtones that most other child behaviors do not, talking with parents about telling lies, cheating, and taking other people's things can be especially challenging. When learning of their child's dishonesty, parents may conclude that the child is somehow flawed. They'll need your help to understand that these mistakes are just that—mistakes—not permanent conditions, and that children can change their behavior with positive support from the adults in their lives.

Knowing how upsetting this information can be, plan how you'll discuss these issues with parents. Avoid using charged words, such as "lying" or "stealing," which can trigger strong reactions in parents. Use neutral words and a matter-of-fact description of the child's actions so parents can approach the issue from a problem-solving, not judgmental, standpoint.

Talking With Parents Whose Child Has Been Dishonest	
Instead of using charged words or generalizations	**Be objective and express a desire to help the child**
"I've caught Caitlin stealing several times. She stole something out of a classmate's backpack and an expensive pen from my desk."	"Last week, Caitlin took a special notebook from someone's backpack and a new pen from my desk. She returned both items, but I want to make sure she understands why taking things is not acceptable. I also want to understand what might be motivating her so that I can help her."
"Andrew lies a great deal. He makes up stories about what great things he's been doing. When someone accuses him of doing something wrong, he never tells the truth about it."	"Last week, Andrew shared that he had gone to Australia for the weekend. He also denied breaking our rules, even when I saw him do that. I want him to feel comfortable sharing about his life and to admit when he makes mistakes. I'd like to explore with you some ideas about how to do that."
"Amber lies about her friends to stir up trouble. She makes things up about one girl to upset another. She causes a lot of chaos with her lies."	"Amber and I have been working on friendship challenges. Last week, one of her friends complained that Amber said something untrue about her to another girl. Amber told me she did that so the other girl would like her more. I want to explore with you some positive friendship strategies she can use."

Some parents may also need help understanding the power of reparation as a logical consequence. If a child took an item and then lost or destroyed it—and you ask her to make reparation—the child, not the parents, should do so. Parents sometimes jump in too quickly to rescue the child by taking on the job of reparation themselves. Encourage parents instead to consider this a teaching opportunity and find ways to let the child shoulder the responsibility, such as by using part of her savings to replace the item or earning the money by doing extra chores at home.

On occasion, parents may be so concerned about their child's struggles with honesty that they seek your advice. Share what you're doing in the classroom. You may also want to offer them some of these tips:

- ➤ ***Tell children that perfection isn't required and mistakes are OK.*** Encourage parents to reflect on how they react when their children make mistakes with truth-telling. Let parents know that when children are overly worried about getting in trouble, they may make up stories to avoid responsibility, cheat to get better grades, or try other deceptions.
- ➤ ***Look for teachable moments.*** Encourage parents to look out for real-life opportunities to show the value of honesty. For instance, if a cashier forgets to charge them for an item, take the child back into the store and show what it looks like to correct this error. Older children can also benefit from parents talking about temptations to cheat on taxes or in other situations and how they resisted those temptations.

TEACHING TIP

Talking With Parents Whose Children Have Had Items Taken

- Be sensitive to their feelings. Express empathy for how distressing the situation is for the child and parents.
- If you know who took the item, let the parent know that reparation will be made. You could say, "We found out who took it. That person is going to return it." Be sure to keep the student's name confidential.
- If you don't know who took the item and it still hasn't been returned, be upfront about this fact. Then, share what you've tried and what you'll be doing next.
- Avoid "blaming the victim," especially if bringing the item to school was against class rules. Don't scold or lecture: "Sheila shouldn't have brought her fancy wallet here anyway." Instead, review with the entire class at a later time what possessions are OK to bring to school and what should be left at home.

- ***Reinforce children's behavior when they're honest.*** Help parents understand the value of reacting positively when their children are truthful, especially if they admit to something they did wrong. A brief acknowledgment is best. For example: "You told the truth about breaking my vase. I know that was hard."

Closing Thoughts

Telling the truth is difficult at times for all of us, not just children. As we try to navigate relationships and take care of our own needs, we may say things that are not completely true. As teachers, our job is to teach children the values of being honest and trustworthy—while also preserving their dignity and being empathetic to their struggles and stumbles.

Key Points

- Children may fib, cheat, or take something in an attempt to feel more significant, because they're not sure how to admit to making a mistake, or because they fear getting in trouble.
- Take proactive steps to teach children what being honest looks, sounds, and feels like and to foster healthy relationships among all students.
- Respond to children's mistakes in being honest by addressing the issue privately and using logical consequences appropriately.
- When talking with parents, approach incidents of dishonesty from a problem-solving perspective, not a judgmental one.

10

Frustrations and Meltdowns

Frustrations and Meltdowns

Learning to Handle Disappointment

Increasingly, I'm hearing from teachers about children who have a hard time bouncing back from the little setbacks that life serves up to everyone. A third grade teacher told me about a fairly typical day in her class, with several children acting unhappy even though nothing major has gone wrong.

During a morning discussion, Alexa raises her hand. When she doesn't get called on, she sighs loudly, puts her head down, and refuses to make eye contact with anyone. During reading workshop, Sean can't find his book and goes to the teacher for help. Because she's working with a small group,

the teacher uses a previously taught signal to show that she can't be interrupted now. Sean starts to cry and calls out, "But I need my book."

Later, at recess, the friends Felicity usually plays with kindly reject her idea of playing *Star Wars* and instead play a game one of them made up. She becomes upset and complains to the recess supervisor that her friends are being mean to her. And so the day goes with Alexa, Sean, Felicity, and others feeling increasingly rattled because things aren't going their way.

It's not unusual for children to have trouble bouncing back quickly when things don't go as they had hoped. But routinely getting upset at seemingly minor setbacks can be a problem. Teachers and classmates may become frustrated with the behavior, causing the student's relationships with them to suffer. If the child spends too much class time being upset, her school performance can diminish as well.

In this chapter, you'll learn why children may be having trouble with small setbacks, how to help them develop coping skills, strategies for responding effectively in their moments of upset, and tips for talking productively with parents of a child struggling to handle setbacks.

About the Focus of This Chapter

Some children in our schools may be experiencing major stresses in their lives. Helping them succeed in the face of such adversity is vitally important and beyond the scope of this chapter. In this chapter, I focus on children's abilities to cope with the everyday setbacks and disappointments they encounter in school.

Why Do Some Children Struggle to Bounce Back?

The ability to handle setbacks is not just a trait that some of us are lucky enough to have in our DNA. Rather, it's a set of skills that children can learn and strengthen. Some children haven't had the coaching or practice they need to build those skills and turn them into habits. Others have come to doubt themselves and their abilities so much, or to have such unrealistic expectations, that they struggle even when they've been taught these skills. Understanding the reasons children struggle with setbacks can help us to remain patient and support them in developing their ability to cope.

Lack of skills needed for handling disappointment

Some children simply haven't been taught how to handle disappointment. They don't know how to put problems in perspective, soothe themselves, or find another option. Every problem is seen as catastrophic. If a classmate politely declines an invitation to play, they might view it as a horrible insult. Once upset, they have few strategies other than crying, fuming, or pouting. They haven't learned that they have the power to chart a new course of action after a setback.

Lack of self-confidence

Many children who get easily frustrated are also discouraged children. They've come to believe that they're not smart enough, or strong enough, or good enough at anything. Even at an early age, they doubt themselves and go to great efforts to avoid taking risks or failing. When, despite those efforts, they do fail, it confirms their low opinions of themselves and they retreat further, cry, or refuse to participate.

Unrealistically high expectations

Some children have unrealistic expectations of themselves, classmates, teachers, and life in general. When people don't act as they had hoped, when events turn out differently from what they had expected, or when they cannot accomplish a task as they had planned, they view these setbacks as major disappointments. Students like these need help learning how to form realistic expectations.

Used to easy success

Some children's life experiences have led them to believe that things should always go their way. Perhaps their parents have tried to shield them from having to face any negative consequences (bringing their homework to school if they forget it, for instance). Or if they want to play a certain game but their friends want to play another, they know to pout until the friends give in.

The longer these children go without having to deal with challenges, the fewer chances they have to develop skills for resilience. Over time, these children may start to doubt their own abilities to cope with even a small challenge.

Desire for attention

Still other children might gain a feeling of significance from the attention they get when they're in distress. They may have learned that when they act upset, people rush to check on them or solve their problems. They might also have discovered that if they appear not to know how to do something, someone else will help them or actually do it for them. These children may feel important only when others provide them with this type of attention.

Unmet physical needs

Lack of sleep or adequate nutrition can also cause or exacerbate children's reactions to disappointments. Children who are overtired or hungry have to use a great deal of energy just to get through the day. When things don't go as they wish, they're much more likely to overreact.

Coping and child development

Although children of all ages can have trouble coping with disappointment, certain child developmental characteristics may increase these challenges.

Some Child Development Characteristics Related to Coping With Disappointment		
Grade	**Characteristic**	**Influences on coping ability**
2nd (ages 6–8)	• Can be inward-looking; sometimes moody or touchy • Need frequent reassurance from adults • Don't like taking risks or making mistakes	• May see problems or situations more negatively than is warranted • May see own mistakes as a sign of lack of ability
4th (ages 8–10)	• Complain frequently • Often feel worried or anxious • Can be moody or negative	• May fear that others will judge them harshly if they fail • May overreact to events and lash out quickly
6th (ages 10–12)	• May be moody or sensitive • Impulsive	• Tend to react dramatically and emotionally to perceived slights, mistakes, or problems • May react quickly without thinking through consequences

While children in the grades listed in the chart may struggle a bit more with setbacks, it's important to teach every child how to deal with life's disappointments. All children need to develop a set of skills that will help them face social and academic challenges with confidence and bounce back. The sections that follow will help you work with children on this crucial skill set.

Children With Chronic Stress, Trauma, Depression, and Anxiety Disorders

These and other serious mental health conditions can make children feel unsafe and on edge much of the time. As a result, they may often be in a "fight or flight" mode, primarily relying on the reactive part of their brain to get by.

We may think it's irrational for a child to cry, for example, when he does not get the pencil he wants, since there are plenty of other pencils available. Rather than processing the experience using the "reasoning" portion of his brain, however, the child may be reacting at a more basic level and be unable to control his behavior in the moment.

If you have reason to believe that a child has a significant mental health condition, consult a school counselor, psychologist, social worker, or administrator. The advice in this book can help the child develop more resilience and other social-emotional skills, but it does not take the place of a comprehensive intervention plan.

Overcoming Everyday Setbacks

Proactive Steps to Build Coping Skills

Students who easily crumple when disappointed need our help developing new skills and habits. They'll also need our patience, because this process takes time. Support their growth by teaching them coping skills one step at a time, preparing them for possible setbacks, and reinforcing their progress in dealing appropriately with disappointment.

Develop positive relationships with students

Students who are working on coping skills need to believe that they're capable people with unique qualities and talents. Take the time to get to know them—their likes, dislikes, strengths—and let them know you know them. This sends a powerful message of how important they are to you and the classroom community.

As you get to know each child, you'll be better able to anticipate situations that may be challenging for them and help them prepare for those. You'll also have a better sense of how each child behaves during a time of upset—whether they're capable of calming down quickly and talking rationally or, instead, need a little comforting and more time to restore themselves to equilibrium. A healthy teacher-student relationship can also help a child feel more motivated to work with you on coping with upsets.

Maintain a predictable routine

As often as you can, follow the same daily schedule and stick to established routines (how you start the day, signal for attention, and so on). Post routines and schedules and clearly mark any deviations. This consistency helps students feel more comfortable and confident.

Also monitor your reactions to changes in the schedule and other surprises. The more even-keeled you are, the more students can rely on you. While you cannot shield students from all unexpected events—nor should you try—you can help them find a level of security at school from which they can develop greater strengths in handling the unexpected.

Prepare students in advance for any changes

When you know students are about to encounter a challenge, such as a tough assignment or change to the daily routine, do your best to prepare them. For instance, before going on a field trip, let students know what to expect—how they'll get there, what they'll do there, what the behavior expectations are—and invite students' questions. You might even practice going on the field trip with students, using Interactive Modeling or role-play. For more on Interactive Modeling and role-play, see pages 24–25.

Teach some basics about how the brain works

All students, not just those who have trouble coping with setbacks, can benefit from a basic understanding of how their brain functions, particularly the differences between the brain's "emotional" and "rational" networks. Even young children can understand that when they're upset, their brain doesn't work in the same way as when they're calm. In particular, help students learn that they can change their emotions by using their brains—when they're upset, they can take steps to calm themselves down. Consider also asking a school counselor to set up a workshop on stress management for your class.

Teach coping skills

Teach skills for handling disappointment and practice them with children in realistic situations.

➤ ***Words for emotions.*** To bounce back from disappointment, children first need to recognize their feelings, especially when they're feeling stressed or upset, so they can apply coping strategies. Through children's literature, games, and direct instruction, teach students the vocabulary to describe their emotions. For young children, display faces express-ing various emotions with simple labels, such as *happy*, *sad*, *frustrated*, *confused*, and *afraid*. For older children, have them make a chart of emotion-related vocabulary words that they can refer to for writing assignments or discussions of a book character's emotions.

➤ ***Appropriate ways to express disappointment.*** Present children with real-life situations and use Interactive Modeling, role-play, and classroom discussions to teach acceptable responses to disappointment. Situations might include:

- not getting called on during a class discussion
- not getting their first choice of a classroom supply or recess activity
- a friend wanting to sit with someone else at lunch
- needing to ask you a question when you're unavailable

Teach these "school-acceptable" ways to respond to such setbacks:

- mild physical reaction (quick downward frown, finger snap, or shrug)
- mild verbal expression ("Drat") or laughing it off
- deep breathing
- respectful disappointment ("That disappoints me because . . .")

➤ ***How to put setbacks in perspective.*** Distinguishing between a minor setback and a major one can be hard for any child, but it's a crucial building block of effective coping. One way to teach this skill is to give students a variety of scenarios and sort them out together. For example:

Smaller Hurdle	Bigger Hurdle
• You don't get called on in class. • You don't get the color of marker you want when you want it. • You lose a game at recess or PE.	• Someone makes fun of you during a class discussion. • You worked hard on an assignment, but someone rips it. • You lose in the championship game.

You can also look for instances of individuals facing hurdles in children's books or historical or current events and discuss these with your class. (See pages 252–255 for a list of helpful children's books.)

➤ ***How to calm down.*** Children who lack coping skills often look to others to comfort them, so they need to learn how to do that for themselves. Teach students strategies such as taking deep breaths, stretching, doing wall push-ups, counting, going for a walk, and talking with a trusted adult. You may want to give children a designated spot or soft chair in the classroom where they can go to calm down when upset. Teach them when and how to use this spot, either as part of teaching time-out or as a separate lesson.

➤ ***Making a different choice.*** It can be very empowering for students to realize that when they don't get their first choice, they can sometimes avoid disappointment by changing their choice. Use teachable moments to help students practice doing this. For example, when there's a limited quantity of a supply that many students want, "freeze" the situation and have students brainstorm how they could change their choices if supplies run out.

Reinforce students' efforts at handling disappointment

Be on the lookout for times when students handled upsets, dealt with challenges independently, or otherwise showed some ability to stay in control when things didn't go as they wished. Reinforce students' efforts even if they reacted inappropriately at first, but then corrected themselves midstream. Follow up with a reflective question to help students figure out what made the difference that time.

Reinforcing Language in Action

If a situation like this happens	Try this
Charlie often gets upset when he's not at the front of the line. Today, he started to complain, but then stopped and quietly stayed put near the end of the line.	"Charlie, I noticed that you stopped yourself from complaining about not being first in line and stayed in your spot. By letting Grace take the front spot, you helped our class get to the art room on time. What helped you do that today?"
Viola usually comes to you whenever she has even a minor problem. Today, when her pencil tip broke, she quietly got up, put it in the "sharpen" box, and took another one out.	"Viola, I saw you getting a new pencil on your own today. What helped you solve this problem independently?"
Sang often has trouble accepting any feedback that he thinks is negative. Today, a friend tells him he's joined the wrong group for a discussion. He smoothly switches to the right group.	"Sang, when Laurence told you that you were a 'five' and his group was the 'fours,' you accepted his correction. How did you keep yourself from getting upset today?"

Model effective coping yourself

Children need to see role models, so when you experience a disappointment, consider sharing it, along with how you moved past it and what you learned. If you encounter a setback at school, model regrouping quickly or taking a moment to breathe deeply, and then moving forward.

When Children Get Rattled

How to Respond Effectively in the Moment

Remember that children develop new skills over time and at different rates. As they develop greater coping skills, they'll make mistakes. The calmer you are when they fail to shake off a little setback as practiced, the easier it will be for them to bounce back.

Keep your cool

We may get annoyed if students get quickly frustrated or seek our help for what we consider minor problems. But when we show our frustration, the child may become more upset, furthering diminishing his sense of competence. If you feel frustrated, take some deep breaths or, if possible, a short break before talking with him about the behavior.

TEACHING TIP

Children Who Overreact to Minor Injuries

When a child who tends to get distraught over seemingly small injuries complains of a horrible pain from a tiny scrape, give him a quick but sincere acknowledgment. For example: "That must hurt" or "What do you think you need?"

Don't give him too much attention. But also refrain from saying something dismissive, such as "That cut? That's nothing. Go play."

Comfort a child who's deeply upset

When you believe a child is in true distress—even if unsure why—give her comfort and support. Whether rational or not, a child who's distraught needs care (a pat on the shoulder or kind words, such as "It's going to be OK") and some time to calm down. While some teachers worry that offering comfort can diminish a child's ability to handle disappointments, not doing so may make a situation worse and damage your relationship with her.

Remind and redirect in a calm voice

If you believe the child is not overly distressed, use a calm voice to remind him of the expectations or to redirect him. Try to offer such reminders or redirection privately to minimize embarrassment.

Reminding and Redirecting Language in Action	
If a situation like this happens	**Try this**
Lydia interrupts your work with a small group during math time to say that she "can't remember" how to complete her assignment.	"Ask a friend for help the way we practiced. Sam looks ready to help. Give me a thumbs-up when you find out what you need." Then, observe and reinforce Lydia's efforts at solving the problem for herself.
Evie asks if she can be the line leader. When you say, "No, that job belongs to Bella today," she gets visibly upset and replies, "I have never even been the line leader before!"	"Evie, stop. Take a deep breath . . . and another. Show me how we practiced responding when you're disappointed." Then, if Evie does so, reinforce with a quick, "That's it!"
At an assembly, the speaker asks for volunteers. T.J. raises his hand, but when he's not picked, he turns around so that his back is to the speaker.	Move closer to T.J. and say, "T.J., turn your body back. Put your eyes on the speaker and show the respectful listening we practiced."

Don't minimize or reason away the upset

The moment a child is distressed is not the time to try to shift her perspective. In the heat of the moment, most children won't be able to reason with you about what they're upset about or why. Instead, use neutral teacher language and logical consequences (see pages 32–34) to help them change direction and restore their emotional balance.

Avoid suggesting that what happened was not worth getting upset about or was insignificant. If you appear to lack empathy, the child may experience the hurt more strongly or for a longer time. After he's calmed down, you may want to revisit the incident to help him gain a different perspective.

Calmly guide the child toward a solution

Instead of trying to convince the child not to be upset or negotiating with her, use neutral language to lay out the options. Then, step back and let the child make the choice. Or, use open-ended questions to help the child figure out what she needs in that moment.

Teacher Language in Action: Guiding Children to Solve Problems Independently		
Situation	**Instead of this**	**Try this**
Devon refuses to participate in a class game unless he can be "It."	"Come on, Devon, if you participate this round, you can be 'It' next round."	"It's up to you whether to participate. We'd like to have you join us, but if you don't want to, you need to follow our rules for 'passing.'"
Emma complains that she needs you to sit with her to do her math.	"I know you can do it. Remember last week when you did problems just like this? You know how good you are at math."	"Tell me more about what you think the problem is." Or, "What kind of help do you think you need?"
You call on someone other than Ani to act out a scene from the read-aloud. She puts her head down and says, "I never get to be the actress."	"That's not true. Remember last week? You acted out the part of Gooney Bird Greene in our social studies dramatization."	"I know you're disappointed. Show me one strategy we practiced for overcoming your disappointment."

Respond with logical consequences, if needed

When a child is so upset that teacher language is not effective, you may need to use a logical consequence to help her regroup and preserve her relationships with classmates (who may feel dismayed by how she's acting). Use a calm, matter-of-fact voice when giving a consequence to keep from further upsetting the child. See the examples that follow.

Logical Consequences in Action	
If a situation like this happens	**Try this**
Marcus is working on a project with three other classmates. He wants to make a poster as the final product, but the other three agree to make a brochure. He starts drumming on the tabletop and refuses to talk when they ask for his help getting started.	**Loss of privilege:** "Marcus, stay here. Eric, Cindy, and Evan, take your materials to the rug area and work there." Give Marcus a few minutes to collect himself. When he's ready, say, "Your group is going to work without you today. We'll talk later about how to get back on track with them. For now, complete this part of the project."
Chloe is working on a writing assignment. She asks Felix to help her spell a word, but he suggests she look for it on the word wall instead. Chloe gets angry and rips her paper.	**Time-out, followed by "you break it, you fix it":** "Chloe, take a break." When she appears calm, say, "There's tape at the writing center. Fix your paper and get back to writing."
Khalil drops his lunch tray near his classmate, Chandra, and milk splatters on her legs. Khalil immediately apologizes, but Chandra yells at him, "You idiot, what's wrong with you?"	**Time-out:** "Chandra, take a break. That's not a respectful way to talk to a classmate." Later, check in with Chandra and practice other strategies she could have used to calm down or other words she could have spoken. You may also want to ask about any reparation she might offer to Khalil. (See page 80 for more on encouraging, but not forcing, an apology.)

After you take care of a situation, continue to assess what's going on with a particular child or the whole class. Based on that assessment, return to the proactive strategies outlined on pages 234–238, and reteach or adjust them as needed.

If a Child Continues to Struggle

Your whole-class teaching of how to handle disappointments, along with your timely responses when children get upset, will go a long way toward helping those who struggle in this area. Still, some children may need additional support. Perhaps they're not yet developmentally ready to integrate these skills, or they're not ready to change long-held habits; perhaps something has happened at home, such as a divorce or job loss, that's strained their ability to handle stress. For students who need additional support, try these ideas.

Provide individual practice

Some children simply need more guided experiences in coping with daily challenges. Meet with these students frequently to give them chances to revisit situations in which they became upset. Discuss and practice how they might handle these differently the next time. If a child resists reflecting on a past incident, talk about ways she could handle possible setbacks in the future.

Providing Friendship Support

Children who become easily upset when frustrated often have trouble forming or maintaining friendships.

You can help by carefully assigning work partners, grouping students at lunch and sitting with them, or even setting up choice times during which you or another adult can support the child and a friend.

Scaffold

Students who have difficulty handling setbacks can't develop the necessary skills overnight. You'll likely need to put extra supports in place while they're still working on them. For instance, you might seat the child close to you so that you can signal him when something potentially upsetting is about to occur or after a setback has occurred. Or you might schedule regular breaks for him so he can do stress-relieving activities.

Alternatively, you may need to adjust expectations for a particular child. For example, while your expectation for most students is that they not interrupt you, you might allow this student to interrupt you on a limited basis, such as one time per fifteen minutes. But remember that scaffolds are temporary and should be removed over time. Continue to raise expectations as children develop greater capacities to cope (for instance, increasing the no-interruption time to twenty minutes or gradually offering fewer stress reduction breaks).

Hold a problem-solving conference

A one-on-one conference in which you share problem-solving responsibility with the child sends a powerful message to him—that you believe he's capable. This belief in one's own abilities is a key to recovering from setbacks. During this conference:

- ***Establish a positive tone*** by connecting around a recent event or topic he enjoys or by pointing out a positive effort or accomplishment.
- ***Explain why his reactions are problematic*** for him and his classmates. For example: "When you slam your books or refuse to talk to anyone for a long time when you're upset, it makes your classmates feel less safe around you, and it keeps you from enjoying school and learning as much as you can."
- ***Explore ideas*** about why he's experiencing these struggles.
- ***Propose some possible strategies*** for diffusing feelings of distress, such as a private signal, a special spot for calming down, or a choice of two ways to deal with setbacks.

Consider an individual written agreement

Some students may continue to have trouble handling minor setbacks even after you've tried several different strategies. For these children, an individual written agreement might help them become more self-aware of their struggles and how they can exert some control of themselves. This agreement provides the child with a concrete goal to work toward, frequent feedback on how she's doing in meeting the goal, and, when appropriate, some extrinsic, nonmaterial reward.

Generally, turn to this strategy after you and the child have tried others and she still seems unable to deal with everyday disappointments. Here's an example of the basic outline of such an agreement:

- ***A clearly defined goal.*** "Sara will react to disappointments in a way that helps her quickly regain self-control and allows those around her to continue their learning." (The teacher and Sara flesh out what such reactions look and sound like when they meet.)
- ***A reasonable standard for success*** in meeting the goal—"Sara will be successful eighty percent of the time."
- ***A way to track success*** that's easy for the student to see and understand—check marks on a chart or craft sticks in a jar, for instance.
- ***A nontangible reward*** for meeting the goal—"If successful, Sara can use a selection of art materials for a project for fifteen minutes before the closing circle."

Consult with other professionals

If a child's problems persist or become more severe despite your efforts, ask for help from an administrator, special education coordinator, school counselor, or other school mental health professional. It may be that the child has deeper issues or needs a more structured and comprehensive plan.

How to Talk With Parents About Frustrations and Meltdowns

The issue of how their child handles disappointment often feels very personal to parents. Some may feel that had they done something differently, their child would now be better able to bounce back from setbacks. Other parents might have a different view of life and not want their child to experience anything going wrong. A few parents may respond defensively and wonder if these problems are due to their child being mistreated by classmates or even by you. Given the emotional nature of the information you need to convey, follow the tips below and the general advice about talking with parents, given on pages 41–44.

Communicate positives beforehand

A key to talking with parents about their child's struggles is to communicate as many positives as you can about their child. Start relaying these early in the year and then from time to time as the year progresses. Hearing that their child is having a hard time dealing with setbacks at school can leave parents with an unsettling image of their child's day. If you've previously conveyed some positive school moments for their child, it's much easier for parents to keep this issue in perspective.

Give your observations objectively

Remember to matter-of-factly describe what you've observed and why it's a problem. Don't try to label or diagnose the problem. Be especially careful not to compare the child to a mythical "norm" or to other children of the same age. Parents are more likely to react defensively to such comparisons and wonder why you're not accepting their child for who he is.

Talking With Parents About Coping Skills	
Instead of labeling or diagnosing	**Try describing observations objectively**
"Brandon loses it whenever things don't go his way. He pouts and tries to make everyone around him feel bad. He's very manipulative and tries to control everyone else through these reactions."	"Brandon and I have been working on some strategies for handling disappointment. Early in the year, he cried if I said 'No' to a request. Lately, he's been yelling at classmates if they don't do what he wants. Let me tell you about what we've been working on this week."
"Annie just can't take it if things go wrong. She needs to learn that life isn't always fair. If she doesn't, she's headed for big disappointments some day. We can't protect her from everything."	"Annie often gets upset when things don't go her way. For example, when she wasn't chosen for the library committee, she stomped her feet and talked about the unfairness of it all day. I'm working with Annie and the class to learn how to express disappointment, soothe themselves, and put setbacks in perspective."
"Lisa's frequent bouts of crying and anger are causing her friends to try to avoid her at all costs. They find her babyish and don't want all the drama she's bringing to recess and lunch."	"Last week, Lisa wanted her friends to swing with her, but they played soccer instead. She cried all recess. I'd like to discuss ideas for helping her express herself more effectively with friends, as well as learn how to compromise and be OK with not getting her way."

If parents ask for your advice

Occasionally, parents may ask for your help in dealing with their child's difficulties coping outside of school. If so, you might want to suggest the following:

- Try to stick to schedules and routines. When possible, prepare the child in advance for variations or potentially upsetting events.
- Avoid "catastrophizing" setbacks or going out of the way to protect the child from disappointment.

- Help the child sort problems into big versus small.
- Make a chart of three possible ways to deal with setbacks for the child to look at as needed.
- Practice with the child some strategies to use in the moment of upset, such as deep breathing.
- Don't try to reason with the child while he's upset.

Closing Thoughts

Children who recover quickly when things don't go their way are able to have happier, more productive days at school. You can help children develop this capacity both through your proactive work and your calm reactions in moments of upset. As with all skills, it may take a while for children to develop coping strategies. And you may need to tap into your own coping strategies when a child slips into old patterns of behavior. But with your dedicated effort and patience, children can eventually learn to take life's routine setbacks in stride.

Key Points

- Bouncing back from disappointment is a set of skills and habits that take time for children to develop.
- Teach and help children practice how to stay calm in moments of distress, such as by using deep breathing, and how to bounce back from disappointments, such as by putting things in a healthy perspective.
- Respond to children's frustration and exaggerated responses to setbacks by staying calm and using matter-of-fact reminders and redirections.
- Describe your observations objectively when working with parents to build up a child's ability to cope. Tell them about their child's positive qualities, not just her struggles.

CONCLUSION

When I decided to be a teacher, Hollywood-inspired images led me to expect magical moments in which students' lives would be transformed before my eyes (hopefully with a great soundtrack in the background). But I quickly came to realize that the results of my efforts were rarely so obvious. The truth is that we teachers do change children's lives, but those changes usually unfold over time, and we may never fully see from moment to moment the positive effects we're having.

But, if we're looking, we can see small signs that our efforts are working. I learned to take note when a child who struggled with including others reached out to a classmate. Or to notice that my class of sillies was learning how to laugh for just a little while and then turn off their giggles. It surprised me how these little behavior changes made such a big difference in the classroom and in my teaching. I also discovered that paying attention to these little changes kept my spirits up day-to-day and bolstered me for the inevitable challenges that did arise.

When we look for overnight, Hollywood-teacher-movie success, we set ourselves and our students up to fail. We're better off keeping track of—and celebrating—the little steps that indicate progress.

What signs of progress are you seeing?

Focus on these incremental steps—and which of your efforts contributed to them—and realize that, little by little, you are making a positive difference in children's behavior and in their lives.

APPENDIX A

Helpful Children's Books

Apologizing

A Ball for Daisy by Chris Raschka (grades K–1)

Forgive Me, I Meant to Do It: False Apology Poems by Gail Carson Levine, illustrated by Matthew Cordell (grades 3–7)

Lilly's Purple Plastic Purse by Kevin Henkes (grades K–3)

Sorry! by Trudy Ludwig, illustrated by Maurie J. Manning (grades 2–5)

This Is Just to Say: Poems of Apology and Forgiveness by Joyce Sidman, illustrated by Pamela Zagarenski (grades 4–6)

Empathy and Perspective-Taking

Anna Hibiscus by Atinuke, illustrated by Lauren Tobia (grades K–3)

The Bedspread by Sylvia Fair (grades 2–4)

Duck! Rabbit! by Amy Krouse Rosenthal, illustrated by Tom Lichtenheld (grades K–3)

My Heart Will Not Sit Down by Mara Rockliff, illustrated by Ann Tanksley (grades K–3)

The One and Only Ivan by Katherine Applegate, illustrated by Patricia Castelao (grades 4–6)

The Other Side by Jaqueline Woodson, illustrated by E. B. Lewis (grades 1–3)

The Teddy Bear by David McPhail (grades K–3)

Two Bad Ants by Chris Van Allsburg (grades 1–6)

Feelings

Cowardly Clyde by Bill Peet (grades 1–4)

Feelings by Aliki (grades K–2)

How Are You Peeling? by Saxton Freymann and Joost Elffers (grades K–3)

Honesty

A Hen for Izzy Pippik by Aubrey Davis, illustrated by Marie Lafrance (grades 1–4)

The Honest-to-Goodness Truth by Patricia C. McKissack, illustrated by Giselle Potter (grades 1–5)

Too Many Tamales by Gary Soto, illustrated by Ed Martinez (grades K–3)

Mistakes

Accidents May Happen by Charlotte Foltz Jones, illustrated by John O'Brien (grades 3–6)

Balloons Over Broadway by Melissa Sweet (grades 1–4)

Mistakes That Worked by Charlotte Foltz Jones, illustrated by John O'Brien (grades 3–6)

Reporting Versus Tattling

Nobody Knew What To Do by Becky Ray McCain, illustrated by Todd Leonardo (grades 1–3)

Trouble Talk by Trudy Ludwig, illustrated by Mikela Prevost (grades 1–4)

Resilience and Persistence

The Boy on Fairfield Street: How Ted Geisel Grew Up To Become Dr. Seuss by Kathleen Krull, illustrated by Steve Johnson and Lou Fancher (grades 3–6)

Clever Jack Takes the Cake by Candace Fleming, illustrated by G. Brian Karas (grades K–3)

Dex: The Heart of a Hero by Caralyn Buehner, illustrated by Mark Buehner (grades K–3)

Happy Like Soccer by Maribeth Boelts, Illustrated by Lauren Castillo (grades K–2)

Max by Bob Graham (grades K–2)

Pete the Cat: I Love My White Shoes by Eric Litwin, illustrated by James Dean (grades K–2)

Pop! The Invention of Bubble Gum by Meghan McCarthy (grades 2–4)

Starry River of the Sky by Grace Lin (grades 3–6)

Respecting and Appreciating Differences

Big Al by Andrew Clements, illustrated by Yoshi (grades K–4)

The Big Orange Splot by Daniel Manus Pinkwater (K–4)

Chicken Sunday by Patricia Polacco (grades 1–4)

Gooney Bird Greene by Lois Lowry (grades 2–5)

Henry and Mudge and the Careful Cousin by Cynthia Rylant, illustrated by Suçie Stevenson (grades K–3)

Odd Velvet by Mary E. Whitcomb, illustrated by Tara Calahan King (grades K–3)

Wonder by R.J. Palacio (grades 5–6)

Silly or Humor-Based Books

Click, Clack, Moo: Cows That Type by Doreen Cronin, illustrated by Betsy Lewin (grades K–2)

The Dunderheads by Paul Fleischman, illustrated by David Roberts (grades 2–6)

I Want My Hat Back by Jon Klassen (grades K–3)

Joey Pigza Swallowed the Key by Jack Gantos (grades 5–6)

Knights of the Kitchen Table (Book #1 in The Time Warp Trio series) by Jon Scieszka, illustrated by Lane Smith (grades 3–5)

Sideways Stories from Wayside School by Louis Sachar, illustrated by Adam McCauley (grades 1–4)

Z is for Moose by Kelly Bingham, illustrated by Paul O. Zelinsky (grades K–2)

Teasing, Exclusion, and Helping Children Who Are Teased or Excluded

Blubber by Judy Blume (grades 4–6)

Each Kindness by Jacqueline Woodson, illustrated by E. B. Lewis (grades K–4)

The Hundred Dresses by Eleanor Estes, illustrated by Louis Slobodkin (grades 2–6)

Just Kidding by Trudy Ludwig, illustrated by Adam Gustavson (grades 3–6)

The Meanest Thing to Say (from the Little Bill series) by Bill Cosby, illustrated by Varnette P. Honeywood (grades K–2)

My Secret Bully by Trudy Ludwig, illustrated by Abigail Marble (grades 2–6)

The New Girl . . . and Me by Jacqui Robbins, illustrated by Matt Phelan (grades K–2)

Say Something by Peggy Moss, illustrated by Lea Lyon (grades 3–6)

Two of a Kind by Jacqui Robbins, illustrated by Matt Phelan (grades K–3)

William's Doll by Charlotte Zolotow, illustrated by William Pène du Bois (grades K–2)

APPENDIX B

Further Resources

All of the recommended practices in this book come from or are consistent with the *Responsive Classroom®* approach to teaching. Developed by classroom teachers and backed by independent research, the *Responsive Classroom* approach emphasizes social, emotional, and academic growth in a strong, safe, and joyful school community. The goal is to enable optimal student learning.

The *Responsive Classroom* approach is associated with increases in student achievement, decreases in problem behaviors, improvements in social skills, and higher-quality instruction. To learn more about the *Responsive Classroom* approach, see the following resources published by Northeast Foundation for Children and available from www.responsiveclassroom.org ▪ 800-360-6332.

Engaging Academics: Offering lessons and assignments that are active and interactive, appropriately challenging, purposeful, and connected to students' interests.

The Language of Learning: Teaching Students Core Thinking, Listening, and Speaking Skills by Margaret Berry Wilson. 2014.

Learning Through Academic Choice by Paula Denton, EdD. 2005.

Guided Discovery in a Responsive Classroom DVD. 2010.

Classroom Management: Setting up and running a classroom in ways that enable the best possible teaching and learning.

Interactive Modeling: A Powerful Technique for Teaching Children by Margaret Berry Wilson. 2012.

What Every Teacher Needs to Know, K–5 series by Margaret Berry Wilson and Mike Anderson. 2010–2011. (Includes one book at each grade level.)

Teaching Children to Care: Classroom Management for Ethical and Academic Growth K–8, revised ed., by Ruth Sidney Charney. 2002.

Morning Meeting: Gathering as a whole class each morning to greet one another, share news, and warm up for the day ahead.

The Morning Meeting Book, 3rd ed., by Roxann Kriete and Carol Davis. 2014.

80 Morning Meeting Ideas for Grades K–2 by Susan Lattanzi Roser. 2012.

80 Morning Meeting Ideas for Grades 3–6 by Carol Davis. 2012.

Doing Math in Morning Meeting: 150 Quick Activities That Connect to Your Curriculum by Andy Dousis and Margaret Berry Wilson. 2010. (Includes a Common Core State Standards correlation guide.)

Doing Science in Morning Meeting: 150 Quick Activities That Connect to Your Curriculum by Lara Webb and Margaret Berry Wilson. 2013.

Morning Meeting Messages K–6: 180 Sample Charts from Three Classrooms by Rosalea S. Fisher, Eric Henry, and Deborah Porter. 2006.

99 Activities and Greetings: Great for Morning Meeting . . . and other meetings, too! by Melissa Correa-Connolly. 2004.

Morning Meeting Activities in a Responsive Classroom DVD. 2008.

Doing Morning Meeting: The Essential Components DVD and viewing guide. 2004.

Sample Morning Meetings in a Responsive Classroom DVD and viewing guide. 2009.

Morning Meeting Professional Development Kit. 2008.

Positive Teacher Language: Using words and tone as a tool to promote children's active learning, sense of community, and self-discipline.

The Power of Our Words: Teacher Language That Helps Children Learn, 2nd ed., by Paula Denton, EdD. 2014.

Teacher Language for Engaged Learning: 4 Video Study Sessions. 2013.

Teacher Language Professional Development Kit. 2010.

Teaching Discipline: Using practical strategies, such as rule creation and positive responses to misbehavior, to promote self-discipline in students and build a safe, calm, and respectful school climate.

Rules in School: Teaching Discipline in the Responsive Classroom, 2nd ed., by Kathryn Brady, Mary Beth Forton, and Deborah Porter. 2011.

Responsive School Discipline: Essentials for Elementary School Leaders by Chip Wood and Babs Freeman-Loftis. 2011.

Creating Rules with Students in a Responsive Classroom DVD. 2007.

Teaching Discipline in the Classroom Professional Development Kit. 2011.

First Weeks of School: Taking time in the critical first weeks of school to establish expectations, routines, a sense of community, and a positive classroom tone.

The First Six Weeks of School by Paula Denton and Roxann Kriete. 2000.

The First Day of School DVD. 2007.

Classroom Organization: Setting up the physical room in ways that encourage students' independence, cooperation, and productivity.

Classroom Spaces That Work by Marlynn K. Clayton with Mary Beth Forton. 2001.

Movement, Games, Songs, and Chants: Sprinkling quick, lively activities throughout the school day to keep students energized, engaged, and alert.

Closing Circles: 50 Activities for Ending the Day in a Positive Way by Dana Januszka and Kristen Vincent. 2012.

Energizers! 88 Quick Movement Activities That Refresh and Refocus, K–6, by Susan Lattanzi Roser. 2009.

16 Songs Kids Love to Sing (songbook and CD) performed by Pat and Tex LaMountain. 1998.

Preventing Bullying at School: Using practical strategies throughout the day to create a safe, kind environment in which bullying is far less likely to take root.

How to Bullyproof Your Classroom by Caltha Crowe. 2012. (Includes bullying prevention lessons.)

Solving Behavior Problems With Children: Engaging children in solving their behavior problems so they feel safe, challenged, and invested in changing.

Solving Thorny Behavior Problems: How Teachers and Students Can Work Together by Caltha Crowe. 2009.

Sammy and His Behavior Problems: Stories and Strategies from a Teacher's Year by Caltha Crowe. 2010. (Also available as an audiobook.)

Working With Families: Hearing parents' insights, helping them understand the school's teaching approaches, and engaging them as partners in their children's education.

Parents & Teachers Working Together by Carol Davis and Alice Yang. 2005.

Child Development: Understanding children's common physical, social-emotional, cognitive, and language characteristics at each age, and adapting teaching to respond to children's developmental needs.

Yardsticks: Children in the Classroom Ages 4–14, 3rd ed., by Chip Wood. 2007.

Child Development Pamphlets (based on *Yardsticks* by Chip Wood; in English and Spanish). 2005 and 2006.

To Learn More:

- Visit www.responsiveclassroom.org for additional information about the *Responsive Classroom* approach to teaching, including the strategies discussed in this book, free articles, blog posts, and video clips.

Resources From Other Publishers

Mindset: The New Psychology of Success by Carol S. Dweck, PhD. Ballantine Books. 2006.

The Optimistic Child: A Proven Program to Safeguard Children Against Depression and Build Lifelong Resilience by Martin E. P. Seligman, PhD. Mariner Books. 2007.

The Respectful School: How Educators and Students Can Conquer Hate and Harassment by Stephen L. Wessler. Association for Supervision and Curriculum Development. 2003.

Setting Limits in the Classroom: A Complete Guide to Effective Classroom Management with a School-wide Discipline Plan, 3rd edition, by Robert J. MacKenzie. Three Rivers Press. 2010.

The Whole-Brain Child: 12 Revolutionary Strategies to Nurture Your Child's Developing Mind by Daniel J. Siegel, MD, and Tina Payne Bryson, PhD. Delacorte Press. 2011.

For Working With More Challenging Behaviors

The Behavior Code: A Practical Guide to Understanding and Teaching the Most Challenging Students by Jessica Minahan and Nancy Rappaport, MD. Harvard Education Press. 2012.

Beyond Time Out: A Practical Guide To Understanding and Serving Students with Behavioral Impairments in the Public Schools, 2nd edition, by John Stewart, PhD. Hastings Clinical Associates. 2002.

Challenging Behavior in Elementary and Middle School by Barbara Kaiser and Judy Sklar Rasminsky. Pearson. 2009.

Challenging Behavior in Young Children: Understanding, Preventing, and Responding Effectively, 3rd edition, by Barbara Kaiser and Judy Sklar Rasminsky. Allyn & Bacon. 2011.

The Explosive Child: A New Approach for Understanding and Parenting Easily Frustrated, Chronically Inflexible Children by Ross W. Greene, PhD. HarperCollins. 2001.

Lost at School: Why Our Kids with Behavioral Challenges Are Falling Through the Cracks and How We Can Help Them by Ross W. Greene, PhD. Scribner. 2009.

ACKNOWLEDGMENTS

I want to begin by thanking and acknowledging a person I don't really know but admire from afar, Ruth Charney. As I embarked on my teaching career, my principal put Ruth's book *Teaching Children to Care* in my hands. I read it cover to cover . . . twice . . . the summer before my first year of teaching. The advice Ruth gave, based on the *Responsive Classroom* approach to teaching, allowed my students and me to thrive that year. And the writer in me was inspired not just by the advice but the way she gave it. She wrote so eloquently and movingly about students and discipline. I still love to reread her writing.

I also want to thank all the students and families who have shared their challenges with me over the years. I was not always as successful as I would have wanted to be in helping them, but I know that whatever I learned about "doing discipline," they were my best teachers.

Thanks also and as always to the many people who have guided me in my career as a teacher-writer-consultant. There are too many to mention, but I do want to pay special tribute to Kathy Woods, Babs Freeman-Loftis, Paula Denton, Gail Ackerman, Farrar Richardson, Marty Kennedy, Molly Darr, and Katherine Pitt. And, of course, my friend, advisor, and cheerleader Lara Webb is a constant source of inspiration.

Lots of teachers and colleagues shared their wisdom and teaching stories with me in the writing of this book. Thanks especially to Mike Anderson, Greg Bagley, Karen Casto, Sarah Fillion, Babs Freeman-Loftis, and Kerry O'Grady. Even if I didn't specifically mention their stories, they helped me think through so many issues in the book and played an important role in its direction. Thanks also to two other colleagues, Carol Davis and Lynn Majewski, for their insights as well. And thanks to Robin Smith who once again shared her children's book expertise and wisdom with me by reviewing and supplementing my list of children's books; Robin is amazing!

The process of producing a book can be somewhat like making sausage—a little messy and hard to bear along the way but hopefully tasty at the end. My editor, Jim Brissette, always makes the process bearable even at its messiest. Alice Yang and Mary Beth Forton do the same by providing their usual strong guidance and vision. Their feedback, as well as that of the readers, Mindy Ryan, Katherine Amy Ross, and Earl Hunter II, made the book richer and more valuable. Caltha Crowe especially pushed me to think more deeply and carefully about what I put on the page as well. And Helen Merena, as always, managed to present the words and pictures in a way that I hope you as readers find as beautiful and inspiring as I do.

While I was writing, I had the joy of having a three-year-old underfoot. Thanks to my son, Matthew, for helping me understand child development from a close vantage point, put some of my own advice to the test, and truly appreciate how precious every child is to their parents and families. And thanks, as always, to my husband, Andy, for supporting me, believing in me, and cheering me on as a writer. To my parents, siblings, nieces, nephews, and in-laws, your ongoing support and love mean a great deal to me always.

ABOUT THE AUTHOR

Margaret Berry Wilson has used the *Responsive Classroom* approach to teaching since 1998. She worked for fifteen years as a classroom teacher in Nashville, Tennessee, and San Bernardino, California, before becoming a *Responsive Classroom* consultant with Northeast Foundation for Children.

Margaret is the author of a number of books published by Northeast Foundation for Children, including *The Language of Learning: Teaching Students Core Thinking, Listening, and Speaking Skills* (2014); *Interactive Modeling: A Powerful Technique for Teaching Children* (2012); *Doing Math in Morning Meeting: 150 Quick Activities That Connect to Your Curriculum* (with co-author Andy Dousis; 2010); and *Doing Science in Morning Meeting: 150 Quick Activities That Connect to Your Curriculum* (with co-author Lara Webb; 2013).

INDEX

ABOUT THE PUBLISHER

Northeast Foundation for Children, Inc., a not-for-profit educational organization, is the developer of *Responsive Classroom*®, an evidence-based education approach associated with greater teacher effectiveness, higher student achievement, and improved school climate. *Responsive Classroom* practices help educators create classrooms characterized by engaging academics, positive community, effective management, and developmentally appropriate teaching. We offer the following resources for educators:

Professional Development Services

- Workshops for teachers and administrators (locations around the country and on-site)
- On-site consulting services to support implementation
- Resources for site-based study
- National conference for school and district leaders

Publications and Resources

- Books and videos for teachers and school leaders
- Professional development kits for school-based study
- Website with extensive library of free articles: www.responsiveclassroom.org
- Free newsletter for educators
- The *Responsive*® blog, with news, ideas, and advice from and educators

For details, contact:

Northeast Foundation for Children, Inc.
85 Avenue A, P.O. Box 718, Turners Falls,
Massachusetts 01376-0718

800-360-6332 ▪ www.responsiveclassroom.org
info@responsiveclassroom.org